PROPHETIC UNTIMELINESS

PROPHETIC UNTIMELINESS

A CHALLENGE TO THE IDOL OF RELEVANCE

OS GUINNESS

HOURGLASS BOOKS

A Division of Baker Book House Co
Grand Rapids, Michigan 49516

© 2003 by Os Guinness

Published by Baker Books
a division of Baker Book House Company
P.O. Box 6287, Grand Rapids, MI 49516-6287
www.bakerbooks.com

Second printing, February 2004

Printed in the United States of America

Scripture taken from *The Revised English Bible* (Oxford: Oxford University Press, 1989). Used with permission.

ISBN 0-8010-1260-0

Library of Congress Cataloging-in-Publication Data is on file at the Library of Congress, Washington, D.C.

DOM
and to
John R. W. Stott
a giant in our generation and a cherished friend

CONTENTS

.

INTRODUCTION

WINSTON CHURCHILL WAS ONCE INVITED to give an address at a college in Canada. The speech was before noon, but his hosts knew that the great man enjoyed his whisky, so they offered him a glass. It was earlier than he was accustomed to drinking, but he did love whisky, so he took it. The waitress then went along the rest of the platform party offering them whisky and, because Churchill had taken some, they all did too—until they reached a local bishop at the end of the line.

Drawing himself up to his full height, the bishop said primly, "I would rather commit adultery than drink whisky."

To which Churchill quipped to the young woman, "Come back, my dear; I didn't realize we were being given a choice."

All too often, public statements by Christian leaders in the last generation have been like the bishop's—earnest and well-intentioned but disastrously comic, foolish, or ineffectual. The skeptics may say, "Who speaks for God?" And the believer may say, with equal feeling, "Who speaks for us?" For much of what doesn't make one laugh makes one weep, and much of what doesn't make one weep makes one angry.

Nothing could be further from the moral urgency of Isaiah, Jeremiah, and the whole prophetic tradition; the heart-stopping wonder of the relevance of the gospel as preached by George Whitefield and

Billy Graham; or the soaring wisdom of the vision of history seasoned by biblical faith as in the writings of St. Augustine.

It would be tempting to cite recent statements by Christian leaders that are as fatuous as they are earnest. Examples abound, from
television evangelists to church-growth consultants to bishops and
theologians, right down to messages on billboards beside churches
and highways. Protestant and Catholic, mainline and evangelical,
elite and unsophisticated—examples can be found across the spec-
trum of the Christian traditions.

Responses to the terrorist attacks on the World Trade Center
and the Pentagon on September 11, 2001, were demonstration
enough. The most notorious of all came in a broadcast conversa-
tion between two television evangelists. The attack, they said, was
God's judgment on the evils of America's recent behavior. And their
claim was plain spoken, refreshingly politically incorrect, and to
those who know the three-century firestorm of the classical Hebrew
prophets, it was theologically plausible too. "Under God" is no
cliché in the Bible. Unquestionably, God judges and punishes certain
behavior.

But almost immediately, in a most unprophetic turn of events,
one of the evangelists took back the judgment with an abject apol-
ogy—before its weight and possible correctness could be assessed.
Such apologies and public retractions were hardly a feature of the
pronouncements by the biblical prophets that began with "This is
the word of the Lord." But they were men whose words were fire
because they had come directly from the Lord and because they were
"men who feared no men." They were moral heroes of the word—
even at a price.

It's sad to say that rarely has the church seen so many of its leaders solemnly presenting the faith in public in so many weak, trite, foolish, disastrous, and even disloyal ways as today. Such leaders do not speak for most ordinary Christians I know. I suspect the press and media invite them to fulfill a stereotype rather than represent a serious position, but again and again for those who hold the faith with all their hearts and minds, the outcome is anger or sorrow.

But this is no time for flogging dead horses. What we need to do is not only explore how this self-inflicted stupidity has happened, but how we can do better in a day that is hungry for a word from God. That practical and constructive outcome, which lies at the heart of reformation and revival, is the real goal of this book.

> *How have we Christians become so irrelevant when we have tried so hard to be relevant?*

Curiously, an embarrassing fact confronts those who inquire into the problem: This monumental and destructive carelessness has coincided exactly with a mania for relevance and reinvention that has gripped the church. So a disconcerting question arises: *How on earth have we Christians become so irrelevant when we have tried so hard to be relevant?* And by what law or logic is it possible to steer determinedly in one direction but end up in completely the opposite direction?

This is exactly the fate of a significant number of the articulate leaders of Western Christendom. After two hundred years of earnest dedication to reinventing the faith and the church and to being more relevant in the world, we are confronted by an embarrassing fact: Never have Christians pursued relevance more strenuously; never have Christians been more irrelevant.

Never have Christians pursued relevance more strenuously; never have Christians been more irrelevant.

Relevance Is Right

Let's be crystal clear at the outset. Relevance is not the problem. If relevance is properly understood—the quality of relating to a matter in hand with pertinence and appropriateness—we who define ourselves and our lives by the good news of Jesus Christ should be, of all people, most relevant. After all, in knowing what we should do, we are called to be like King David's men, "skilled in reading the signs of the times." We are not to be like the Pharaoh of Jeremiah's day, whom the prophet dismissed as "King Bombast, the man who missed his moment."

Our challenging task is to be like David himself, who was said to "serve God's purpose in his generation." We are to be shaped and directed by the unique biblical view of "time," "generation," "hour," and "moment," with its decisive difference from the contrasting eastern and secularist views. God forbid that Jesus should have cause to weep over our generation as he did over Jerusalem, because we missed our moment.

Indeed, relevance is at the very heart of the gospel of Jesus and is the secret of the church's power down through history. For example, witness the testimony of some of the world's greatest thinkers, writers, scientists, poets, painters, and reformers—Augustine, Dante, Pascal, Rembrandt, Newton, Wilberforce, and Dostoyevsky. Each of them was as faithful to Christ as he was fresh in his times.

In itself the good news of Jesus is utterly relevant or it is not the good news it claims to be.

The gospel is good news. In fact it is "the best news ever" because it addresses our human condition appropriately, pertinently, and effectively as nothing else has, does, or can—and in generation after generation, culture after culture, and life after life. Little wonder that the Christian faith is the world's first truly universal religion and in many parts of the world the fastest growing faith, and that the Christian church is the most diverse society on planet earth, with followers on all continents, in all climates, and under all the conditions of life and development. Of course, Christians can make the gospel irrelevant by shrinking and distorting it in one way or another. But in itself the good news of Jesus is utterly relevant or it is not the good news it claims to be.

So let no one misunderstand or misrepresent this inquiry. There is no merit whatsoever in irrelevance, mere reaction, or being out of date. We who follow Jesus must always be relevant because we must always be bringing him to every new person and situation we encounter. Down the running centuries the new wine has called for countless new wineskins and endless creativity and innovation. The decisive question, which we will be exploring specifically in part 3, is how do we achieve that relevance?

The stakes, of course, are high. The sorry irrelevance of the church in the West is thrown into sharp relief by our world and our historic moment. For better or worse, Western civilization is the most powerful civilization in the modern world and the Christian faith is the single strongest set of ideas that has made the West the West. But at both the elite and the popular levels, and among all traditions of the Christian community, the church is largely irrelevant to Western affairs at a supremely important moment. For today the forces of globalization unleashed by the West are simultaneously stimulating other civilizations (such as the Chinese, Indian, and Islamic) into life while undermining the authority of Western beliefs in the West itself.

Our crying need is to be faithful as well as relevant.

How can this mammoth irrelevance be? Is it simply a coincidence—other reasons are really to blame, we have been unfortunate to be caught at the wrong moment of history, and no amount of relevance would have made us relevant in a declining civilization? Or is there a deeper connection that we should have seen in advance—a plain and simple link between our irrelevance and our pursuit of relevance?

Certainly there are other reasons, which I and others have discussed elsewhere. But in this short book I want to pinpoint the special irony of the latter:

> *By our uncritical pursuit of relevance we have actually courted irrelevance; by our breathless chase after relevance without a matching commitment to faithfulness, we have become not only unfaithful but irrelevant; by our determined efforts to redefine ourselves in ways that are more compelling to the modern world than are faithful to Christ, we have lost not only our identity but our authority and our relevance. Our crying need is to be faithful as well as relevant.*

My concern is constructive rather than critical. The need of the moment is not simply to attack a problem but to embody a vital and practical response. The world needs such an answer and the gospel deserves and requires it. Thus for followers of Jesus Christ at this extraordinary moment in history, it is time to challenge the idol of relevance, to work out what it means to be faithful as well as relevant, and so to become truly relevant without ever ending up as trendy, trivial, and unfaithful.

Homo-up-to-datum *Is a Dunce*

You may ask, what is wrong with pursuing relevance? As so often, the force that affects our thinking is an age-old one that the modern world has reinforced to the point of grotesque distortion. What I am referring to here is our understanding of time, specifically our attitudes to the past, the present, and the future. Obviously, these three aspects of time are related like the three panels of a triptych. In the poet Tennyson's line, "Today is yesterday's tomorrow and tomorrow's yesterday."

Our knowledge of each of them, however, is different. According to traditional wisdom, the past is the easiest and most important part of time to understand, the present the most difficult, and the future quite impossible. But under the influence of the modern world we have reversed this wisdom—generally ignoring the importance of the past, exaggerating our knowledge of the present, and presuming to speak accurately of the future when quite simply we can't.

Most people in most periods are simply happy to follow along behind their times.

Take the case of our distortion of the present. Raymond Aron, the French political theorist, once remarked that very few people are contemporaries of their own time. Most people in most periods are simply happy to follow along behind their times. The significance of our own day dawns for us slowly, if at all, and is usually delivered rather than discovered, second hand at best. Realism rather than humility ensures that for most of us this is likely to remain the situation. The poet Samuel Taylor Coleridge wrote similarly in the nineteenth century, "The great majority of man live like bats, but in twilight, and know and feel the philosophy of their age only by its reflections and refractions."

In the same vein, the great Swiss historian Jacob Burckhardt warned in his *Reflections on History* that we must never forget "the acoustic illusion in which we live." For one thing, there is a huge gap between knowledge and opinion—and ours is an age that is short on knowledge and long on opinion (and the cult of statistics and opinion polling). For another thing, we can never rid ourselves of "the worst enemy of knowledge"—our own views of our own time and personality. As Burckhardt said, "The clearest proof of it is this: as soon as history approaches our own century and our worthy selves, we find everything more 'interesting'; in actual fact it is we who are more 'interested.'"

"Mirrors were invented that man might know himself," the Roman philosopher Seneca said. But put simply, as historian Arnold Toynbee has said, someone trying to understand the present is like a man with his nose pressed against a mirror trying to see his whole body.

The paradox of modern life is that it pretends to relieve this problem for us even as it makes it worse. On the one hand, modern communication holds out the offer of "instant total information," or "total information awareness." Surely it is now possible to be in touch with everything that matters to us, and therefore to be more relevant than ever before. But on the other hand, the outcome of instant, total information is inflation—when more and more of anything is available, less and less is valuable. The net result is that we have produced what historian Daniel Boorstin calls "homo-up-to-datum." But, as he adds tartly, "homo-up-to-datum is a dunce."

This exaggeration of our understanding of the present is only the beginning of the problem. Distortions of our understanding of the future are even worse, not least because they also shape our attitudes to the present. But this leads us back to our original question with a deepened vigilance: *How are we to be wise and understanding, not simply well-informed with a surplus of facts and figures? How are we to be always timely, never trendy? How are we to be redefined—but in the right way?* Clearly, the modern world with all its stunning gifts of communication makes our problem harder, not easier. So we are back to the original challenge with a modern twist.

How are we to be always timely, never trendy? How are we to be redefined— but in the right way?

The urgent task for followers of Jesus is to be truly relevant to our times. The church in the first, fourth, twelfth, sixteenth, and nineteenth centuries may have been magnificent in one way or another, but we are not first-, fourth-, twelfth-, sixteenth-, or nineteenth-century Christians. We are twenty-first–century Christians who must constantly define ourselves by the gospel and remain faithful to Jesus Christ in the twenty-first century. Only then will we be truly relevant.

We therefore need to examine the modern promise of relevance and reinvention. Could it be the means to advance the good news to a confused, weary, and battered world that is hungry for news that is genuinely good? Or is it a Trojan horse that we wheel into the camp at our peril?

Progress through Resistance

The answer, I suggest, is to realize the timeliness of untimeliness: to regain the courage of "prophetic untimeliness" and develop the art of "resistance thinking" and so become followers of Jesus who have the courage to become "untimely people" despite the mesmerizing lure of the present age and its fixation with the future. But how am I using these words?

> *Nietzsche saw that independent thinkers would always be out of step with the conventional wisdom of their generation.*

Prophetic untimeliness is a term adapted from the philosopher Friedrich Nietzsche but shaped by the precedent of the Hebrew prophets rather than the German iconoclast. Nietzsche saw that independent thinkers would always be out of step with the conventional wisdom of their generation. Rather than thinkers of today, caught in the toils of fashion and conformity, they would be thinkers of tomorrow and the day after tomorrow.

In short, he wrote in *Untimely Meditations*, they would be "untimely men: their home is not in this age but elsewhere." They would have the greatest discernment and the most enduring vision born of a different perspective and commitment. Of course, in contrast to Nietzsche, the north star of such independent thinking for the Hebrew prophets was neither their individual genius nor their social stubbornness but "the word of the Lord."

Resistance thinking is a term adapted from a 1945 essay by C. S. Lewis on "Christian Apologetics." It is a way of thinking that balances the pursuit of relevance on the one hand with a tenacious awareness of those elements of the Christian message that don't fit in with any contemporary age on the other. Emphasize only the natural fit between the gospel and the spirit of our age and we will have an easy, comfortable gospel that is closer to our age than to the gospel— all answers to human aspirations, for example, and no mention of self-denial and sacrifice.

"Progress is made only into resisting material."   — C. S. Lewis

---

But emphasize the difficult, the obscure, and even the repellent themes of the gospel, certain that they too are relevant even though we don't know how, and we will remain true to the full gospel. And, surprisingly, we will be relevant not only to our own generation but also to the next, and the next, and the next. C. S. Lewis observed that the same principle holds true in both faith and science: "Progress is made only into resisting material." Resistance thinking, then, is the way of relevance with faithfulness.

Sadly, the word in these paragraphs that causes the most discomfort is *prophetic*. "Prophets are the plague of today, and perhaps of all time, because it is impossible to tell a true prophet from a false one," the Jewish writer Primo Levi wrote. "I don't believe in prophets, even though I come from a heritage of prophets." Doubtless we are right to be wary of false prophets, because the modern parade of counterfeits is as long as the list of true ones is short. In many Christian circles, "prophetic" is shorthand for uncheckable charismatic hunches or for any left-wing, radical critique of the status quo.

But the place of the prophet as the one who speaks the word of the Lord is too important to give up, even with the threat of counterfeits. We might distinguish capital-P "Prophets" from small-p "prophets." The former are those, like Isaiah and Jeremiah, who have heard a direct, explicit, supernatural word from God and can legitimately say, "This is the word of the Lord." The latter are those who interpret their life and times from a biblical perspective and therefore "read the signs of the times" with greater or lesser skill, but never presume the authority and infallibility of "This is the word of the Lord."

> *Our modern view of relevance has been badly skewed by our modern fascination with the future.*

In this second and more modest sense we are all called to be prophets—interpreting events from the perspective of faith and under the aspect of eternity, and always with an eye to what we should *do*, not simply know. We may be wrong when we speak in this way, and we must always be open to correction, but we have the right and the duty to set things forth as we see them under God.

So what is the deeper problem of discernment we are up against in the modern world? It can be stated simply: *Our modern view of relevance has been badly skewed by our modern fascination with the future, which is itself the bastard child of our clock culture that is at the core of the modern world.* Like a fish unable to appreciate the water in which it swims, we take our modern view of time as natural and self-evident. But it isn't. It's highly unusual; partly helpful, partly harmful. We therefore need to stand back in order to view our situation from a wider perspective, so to assess what is human and good, and what is not.

In part 1, we explore the character of modern clock culture, showing how it arose and how it shapes our lives as modern people. In part 2, we will look more closely at its impact on the church and its thinking, and in particular how it shapes the current craze for relevance among many Christians. In part 3, we examine what it takes to resist these distortions with integrity and to count the cost of faithfulness.

Timely Untimeliness

Can we really escape the parochialism of our modern views of time and reassert the importance of humanness as well as Christian faithfulness in the teeth of today's world? Here is where our current Christian irrelevance and marginality actually works in our favor. We have no stakes in the current status quo, so we can think and act without encumbrance. Then, by virtue of the fact that faith gives us an Archimedean point of leverage outside of history and society, we can be strengthened rather than weakened by our marginal position in the power centers of the modern world.

We followers of Jesus are therefore far better situated to undertake such a vital resistance movement today than we were a century ago when we were the unspoken establishment throughout the Western world.

Our timeliness lies in the untimeliness of rejecting modern timeliness.

A catch-22 confronts us, however. Our timeliness lies in the untimeliness of rejecting modern timeliness. Our moment and our hour depend upon our turning from the spurious models of the modern world to the real moment and the real hour seen only under God. But we need to be aware that the gain in perspective is a gain in pressure. As we will see, relevance with faithfulness has a steep cost, but those prepared to pay it win the prize of true relevance.

In his novel *In Light of India*, Octavio Paz writes, "I believe that the reformation of our civilization must begin with a reflection on time." No less is true of the church of Jesus Christ in the West at the beginning of the twenty-first century, and this book is written for those for whom that reformation is a supreme concern and desire.

PART ONE

THE TOOL THAT TURNED INTO A TYRANT

ONE

FACES OF THE
SINISTER GOD

T HE PRESENT CLASH OF CULTURES in the world makes this an
ideal time to see ourselves in the West as we might not have
done earlier. For example, the first months after the September 11
terrorist attacks were like a crash course in the history of the rela-
tionship between the West and Islam. Various dates were flashed
across the screen of public consciousness: 732 and the battle of Tours
when the Islamic tide almost reached to the gates of Paris; 1492 and
the defeat of the Moors in Spain; September 11, 1683, when the last
Muslim forces were repulsed at the siege of Vienna; and 1798 when
General Napoleon Bonaparte landed in Egypt and subjected the
heartlands of the Muslim world to Western military dominance.

But in fact the real conquest of the Near East began far earlier,
and the conqueror was neither a crusader, nor a general, nor a diplo-
mat, nor a missionary. Interestingly, it was a Western machine. And
in fact, it has been called "the mother of machines" and even "the
ultimate missionary machine." I am speaking of the clock. Perhaps
surprisingly, we need to understand the clock to understand our own
position in the church today, for the clock has colonized its Western
inventors as much as people in the rest of the world to whom we
have taken it.

The mechanical clock was invented in Europe around A.D. 1400.
It was pivotal to the rise of the modern world and therefore to mod-

ern consciousness and the impact of the modern world on the rest of the world. "The clock did not man make," an African saying runs. But the clock was certainly instrumental in the making of modern man and woman. Not only is it infinitely more influential than often-cited carriers of globalization such as Coca-Cola, McDonald's, and MTV. But it is the catalyst—or culprit—behind the pressures of modern time on us, and on our views of the present and the future.

By and large the Muslim world was resistant and slow to adapt to mechanical clocks, just as the Chinese welcomed them at once but kept them as toys for the emperor rather than as tools for the whole of society. In the seventeenth century, the English diarist John Evelyn quotes a traveler as saying that the Persians "had neither clocks nor watches." As late as 1947, a French visitor to the Near East remarked that he made a point of being late for appointments on the advice of his hosts, who said, "Here the sky is too blue, the sun too hot. Why hurry? Why do injury to the sweetness of living?"

"Westerners are people with gods on their wrists."   — *Filipino saying*

Today, when globalization is bringing the modern Western view of time to the whole world, the contrast between traditional and modern views is captured in a hundred homespun sayings from people outside the West. Filipinos, for instance: "Westerners are people with gods on their wrists." Or Kenyans: "Westerners have watches but no time. Africans have time but no watches." It is precisely this modern view of time, which I will refer to as "clock time," that we must understand if we are to escape its worst effects while simultaneously reasserting the importance of humanness as well as faithfulness.

Choice and change are at the very heart of the modern world. From manufacturers to marketers, from smorgasbords to supermarkets and shopping catalogs, choice is paraded before us in an endless variety of ways. So when it comes to clocks and watches, we are so used to our options that we don't notice the things over which we have no choice. Do you want a Rolex, an Omega, or a Swatch? A watch that is analog or digital? A traditional or a contemporary style? A watch that's self-winding or battery-driven? Do you want it to be gold or stainless steel? Do you want your alarm to ring or play music? Do you want to wake up at once or to be able to press the snooze button?

In areas like these the choices go on and on, with the only constraints being those of money and fashion. Choice, after all, is the birthright of the modern consumer. But options such as these are actually the trivial faces of modern time. Far more important are the features we can neither choose nor change. In particular, for better or for worse, three features of modern clock time decisively shape our lives and our thinking. Here, as so often, we must understand if we are to withstand.

Precision

The first feature of modern clock time is *precision*. Time and space are the two basic elements in which we live and move as human beings. So the measurement of time is essential to human life as we master nature and take control of our world. Of course, there were ways to measure time before the invention of the clock. But this measurement was largely seasonal, spiritual, and imprecise.

Three important developments lie behind our modern sense of time:

First, the shift from the lunar calendar, which depended only on observation, to the solar calendar, which depended on calculation.

Second, the shift from a natural sense of time, as in days, to an artificial sense of time, as in weeks.

Third, the shift from a sense of periods, as in A.M. and P.M., to a sense of precision, as in hours, minutes, and seconds.

But the decisive development in the rise of the modern world was the invention of the mechanical clock. All the various instruments in use before it were slow and restricted. For instance, without the sun, there was no sundial—which made it useless at night and limited in effectiveness in countries with short days or bad weather. Needless to say, this gave the Greeks and the Italians a great advantage over the Norwegians and the Scots. Equally, the slightest leak or irregular flow in the water clock made it unreliable or put it out of action. And obviously the hourglass had to be turned over exactly as the last grain of sand ran from the top to the bottom if it was to mark more than one hour with any accuracy.

All this was changed by the clock. Not only was the mechanical clock the first important all-metal machine, but it was an instrument for all seasons, all weathers, and all hours of the day and night. Above all, as the technology of the early devices called escapements was replaced by pendulums and then main springs and finally by digital movements with atomic accuracy, the clock became a force for precision that was quite new in human history.

Whether measuring in light years or nanoseconds, we can now measure anywhere and everywhere in the entire universe. The result is a split-second precision in timing that the traditional world would have found astonishing. Precise time is a universal means of measurement and one of the greatest innovations in the entire history of humankind.

Naturally, we modern people take this precision for granted just as we take in the air we breathe. Ours is a world in which lawyers and psychiatrists charge by the hour, telephone companies bill by the minute, television networks charge advertisers by the second, Olympic athletes win or lose by hundredths of a second, and astronauts execute their life-and-death maneuvers in nanoseconds.

In our world of modern precision, punctuality has become a virtue in its own right, and unpunctuality a vice.

Whenever we need and want to be, we can be precise, precise, precise. And in this world of modern precision, punctuality has become a virtue in its own right, and unpunctuality a vice—at least for most people.

Coordination

The second feature of modern clock time is a central consequence of precision—*coordination*. As a moment's thought makes obvious, a precise sense of time is essential not only to science and technology.

It is influential for ordinary life, above all in planning and coordinating our daily affairs. Much of the best and most basic in our daily lives pivots on timing—getting up in the morning, meeting friends, keeping appointments, catching planes, fulfilling deadlines, expecting deliveries, watching the news, or arriving at the church on time. No ancient religious devotee could rival us modern people in our instant, total obedience to the "gods on our wrists" that send us scurrying from one appointment to the next.

It is even said that a central feature of the Western world is our polyphony—the harmony we achieve through balancing unity and diversity, and through blending different parts to give them a common purpose. Such polyphony can be heard in our music (for example, in choirs), in our politics (for example, in different parties under law), and in our sports (for example, with keen rivals competing within the same rules).

The key component of this coordination is clock time, for clock-time precision is what makes possible the plans, schedules, timetables, and logistics of the modern world. For an earlier generation the supreme symbols of this new coordination was the railway and its timetable. Suddenly the nineteenth-century world exploded and contracted at the same time. Whole continents were crisscrossed with lines of communication called railway tracks and little puffing engines ran to and fro industriously according to giant station clocks and weighty timetables. Swiss trains, for example, have always run with the smoothness, efficiency, and cleanliness of Swiss watches. Their coordination is so smooth and efficient that they represent the highest standards of precise coordination.

In our day airports have often replaced train stations, computers have taken over from station masters and timetables, atomic accuracy has done away with ponderous Victorian timepieces, and we are awash with jargon such as "access," "connectivity," and "networking." But when things go well we still say that "they run like clockwork."

Pressure

The third feature of modern clock time is the one about which we are most aware—*pressure*. Today at the high noon of modern life, time in the clock-driven world has become so precise and coordinated that it's all around us, driving us from behind, pulling us from in front, pressing us from above, and squeezing us from both sides. The gods on our wrists have become, in the words of Charles Baudelaire, "the sinister god." As the nineteenth-century French poet protested in his poem "The Clock," "3,600 times per hour, the second whispers: Remember!"

Time has become so precise and coordinated that it's all around us, driving us from behind, pulling us from in front, pressing us from above, and squeezing us from both sides.

If we want to, we can still speak of "killing time" or "doing time"—the first phrase meaning a voluntary and the second an involuntary passing of time when time's passage is its only object. But for most of us, such moments are rare. In fact, after childhood there are very few periods when the clock goes too slow and far too many when it goes too fast. To be sure, a few sharp observers saw the effects of measured time and protested early on. The Roman playwright Plautus, for example, wrote in 200 B.C.,

> The gods confound the man who first found out
> How to distinguish hours! Confound him, too,
> Who in this place first set up a sun dial,
> To cut and hack my days so wretchedly
> Into small portions.

Two millennia later, we can all sympathize with the poet. Time-drivenness is our reality. "Harried and hurried" is now our way of life. "Fretting and fussing" has become our chronic condition. Six centuries after the invention of the clock, the idea of time-keeping has become a euphemism; the idea of time-saving a joke. The tick-tock of the clock has become the background drum-beat and staccato bark of the drill sergeant who drives us across the parade ground of life.

The tick-tock of the clock has become the background drum-beat and staccato bark of the drill sergeant who drives us across the parade ground of life.

No wonder ours is a marginless world of "24 x 7 x 365" living. In 1751, novelist Henry Fielding was the first to write that "time is money." Today time is big money and scarce money. So we "buy time," "maximize time," and make sure we are having "quality time." We figure out the "opportunity costs" of all we do. We become adept at "multi-tasking." We press life to the edges and make the most of every spare second we have—with "split-screen news" packing in the information for us, "on-hold advertising" filling in the empty seconds, and "professional queuers" standing in line to save us from the unwanted tax on our time that bureaucrats love to impose.

Time is the ultimate credit card; speed is the universal style of spending.

In our world, a lot happens all the time, so much so that we not only expect it, we require it. Change has to be unceasing, voices have to be rudely grabbing, and the latest has to be replaced instantly by the newest latest. All this has gone so far and become so natural that for many people jam-packed eventfulness is a necessity and attention deficit disorder a common condition.

If it were possible, time and motion experts would like to rationalize every last second of our days so that we could be even more efficient and productive—even in our leisure. At the beginning of the age of mass-production, Henry Ford said of his ideal worker, "He must have every second necessary, but not a single unnecessary second." Was he being generous or ruthless? It all depends on the standard by which he judged what was necessary.

But the underlying modern attitude to time is plain: pressure, pressure, pressure. Too much fast food may lead to the "slow-food movement" and wall-to-wall busyness to a sharp rise in time-out practices such as meditation. But the latter are only reactions and diversions. The central thrust of mainstream time-pressure is unrelenting and unstoppable.

Time is the ultimate credit card, speed is the universal style of spending, and "the faster the better" is the ideal tempo of life. Call it "craziness," call it "the curse of our age," call it "the tyranny of the urgent," call it anything you like. But it is impossible to stop the world today even if you want to get off—and this manic speed is affecting our faith as much as our blood pressure.

THE TYRANNIES
OF TIME

G EORGE ORWELL ONCE SAID, "We have now sunk to the depth
where the restatement of the obvious is the first duty of intel-
ligent men." In a much more trivial way, all we were really doing in
the last chapter was putting into words what we already instinctively
know. Features of modern time such as precision, coordination, and
pressure are obvious once we pause to think about them—though
we rarely do. That is what time in the modern world is like, and
that is how it hits us and shapes us.

Describing modern time has a certain value, but we have to go
further. There are deeper features that we must delve into. They are
not as obvious as the ones we have just looked at, but they are just as
vital. In fact, they are the real tyrannies of time in our world, and
they are especially important for untimely people seeking to think
independently and live with integrity.

The Power of Labeling

The first deeper consequence of our modern view of time is its *power
in labeling,* or *in defining reality.* Words are handles or labels that we
stick on reality. They are greatly influential because the way we *say*
things shapes the way we *see* things. Say something often enough
and eventually we'll come to see it that way. Before long even something fresh and startling will become routine and self-evident. Our

use of nicknames and name-calling are obvious examples of the use of words to exert power. Call someone a "beanpole" or a "dummy" and people aren't likely to expect them to be overweight or blessed with a surfeit of gray cells.

Say something often enough and eventually we'll come to see it that way.

The words we use to speak about time are no exception. And they are all the more powerful because they go unnoticed. Embedded in our daily language, they shape and furnish our view of time and thus direct and mold our experience of time itself. For instance, one of the strongest effects of the clock was the way that even the universe began to be seen as one gigantic clock. In the words of the seventeenth-century scientist Robert Boyle, at the birth of early modern science the universe was "a great piece of clock work." Modern views have replaced this early modern view, but the powerful, subliminal impact of clocks and clock-time still moves through our language to shape our view of reality. It may be heard at two points in particular.

From Space to Time

One point is the way in which words that once referred to space now refer to time. The word "civilized," for example, used to have a spatial element at its core. A key to the distinction between civilized and uncivilized used to be the idea of being "beyond" in terms of space. If some group saw itself as civilized, then those beyond the circle of their society were the uncivilized. They were "beyond the pale." Most famously the Greeks saw themselves as civilized, while all who were outside the circle of their enlightenment were "barbarians." This measuring stick has been transformed by the rise of clocks and clock time. The uncivilized are no longer *beyond* in terms of space but *behind* in terms of time. They are no longer barbarians but "primitives," "reactionaries," and "Neanderthals"—or in teenage parlance, "retarded." The means of measurement is now one of years and periods rather than miles and boundaries. As advertisers at the turn of the new millennium said archly in a show of chronological snobbery, highlighting the new by scorning the old and passé, "That was so twentieth century."

Another example of words that now refer to time rather than space is the term "progress." In its early use it referred to space, but now it almost always refers to time. Thus John Bunyan's "pilgrim's progress" meant a journey and a king's "progress" once meant a royal procession or parade along a road—more like the movement of a carnival float or a Macy's Thanksgiving Day parade than a scientific discovery or a growth in proficiency or maturity. The latter, of course, would be more common today. "Progress," "progressive," and their opposites, "reactionary," "passé," and "old-fashioned" are more likely to refer to advances or setbacks in science, technology, and civil rights—and always movement in terms of time rather than space.

Prescription, Not Description

The powerful, subliminal impact of clocks and clock time can be heard at a second point—the way in which words smuggle in evaluation in the guise of description. They pretend to describe, but in fact they praise or disparage. This is already clear in the examples above. "Progress" purports to describe an advance but it also pronounces it good. The evaluation is mixed in with the description and it's impossible to take it back.

---

*Words pretend to describe, but in fact
they praise or disparage.*

For those who subscribe to "progressivism"—and in a sense we are all progressives now—progress by definition is good, always good, self-evidently good, unquestionably good. Reaction, by definition, is bad. The world is getting better and better. Whatever *is* is not only right but a great deal better than what was. And of course, whatever is next must be a great deal better still. The word "progress" simply makes it so and tells us so. We are not asked to think. We are not even given the opportunity or the criteria to judge for ourselves. If it's progressive, by definition it must be good. If it's reactionary, it obviously must be bad, and that's the end of it. Discussion over.

The same power of smuggled judgments can be heard in words describing periods of history. For example, the standard labels "Dark Ages/Middle Ages/Modern Age," were first used in the early days of the modern era. To any of us who doesn't know these ages as the historian does, the suggestion is clear. There was very little of worth in the earlier period, and the value of the second period is that it leads to the climax of all the developments, the modern era.

In other words, all roads lead to Rome and all periods point to us. Just keep saying the words and their power will flatter us into believing them. After all, if the latest is the greatest, we in this generation are the consummation of the ages. We are the apex of history. Clearly the purpose of history is us. The present is the occasion to break out the champagne and toast ourselves.

Presumption

The second deeper consequence of our modern view of time is *presumption*. Our modern words about time have a preference and a bias, but the preference is left unstated and the bias unargued. Like an emperor whose writ is absolute within his empire, the unexamined tyranny of modern time imposes its perspectives and preferences on all who live within its sway. Surely and beyond all question, it suggests, this way of seeing things is quite simply the way things are.

Like an emperor whose writ is absolute within his empire, the unexamined tyranny of modern time imposes its perspectives and preferences on all who live within its sway.

The word *progress* is also a clear example of presumption. Needless to say, such terms as progress and decline are perfectly legitimate if they are based on standards by which they can be judged—in other words, on conceptions of the good, the true, and the beautiful. By such standards, which will vary for different people, we are able to judge what is progress and what is decline as based on those standards for those people. But this is not what happens with modern references to progress and decline.

The modern world has such a bias for change that it refers only to bare change and change for change's sake. Any kind of change is enough to qualify as progress. If there is change at all, we can downplay any continuity between the old and the new and discount any talk of criteria with which to evaluate the change. Is the change for the better or for the worse? That's irrelevant. All that matters is change. Progress is change and change is progress, and that's an end of it.

Utopianism is bloated with such unexamined presumption. For example, Edward Gibbon, author of the eighteenth-century classic *The History of the Decline and Fall of the Roman Empire,* made this famous claim:

> It may be safely presumed that no people, unless the force of nature is changed, will relapse into their original barbarisms. . . . We may therefore acquiesce in the pleasing conclusion that every age of the world has increased, and still increases, the real wealth, the happiness, the knowledge, and perhaps the virtue, of the human race.

Like all good Enlightenment thinkers of his time, Gibbon saw the glass fuller all the time. After all, the "force of nature" had decreed it. But reality often shows up the hollowness of such idealism. Gibbon died in 1794 during the Reign of Terror that followed the French revolution, an atrocity that was considered the epitome of evil prior to the Holocaust. The blunt fact was that in both the Reign of Terror and the Holocaust, civilized nations not only "relapsed into barbarism" but exceeded it in the malignancy of their evil.

Clearly, Gibbon's Enlightenment presumption about inevitable progress through "the force of nature" was sadly off the mark. But from the eighteenth century to the 1960s, when the poisonous effect of utopianism had become too disastrous to ignore, the mere incantation of such words as progress, improvement, and amelioration was enough to inspire confidence and assure the world of the broad and sunlit uplands just over the next hilltop.

Today, after a century in which hundreds of millions of people were slaughtered in the name of grandiose ideologies of utopianism, the presumption of this view of progress is under closer scrutiny. Above all, we can see that for all their exaltation of reason, Enlightenment thinkers showed little sense of self-criticism in their philosophy.

> *"He said things that were both true and new; but unfortunately what was true was not new, and what was new was not true."* — *Richard Sheridan*

Far better to have thought critically all along as playwright Richard Sheridan did in a speech to the House of Commons during the same generation as Gibbon. In criticizing another Member of Parliament, he remarked: "He said things that were both true and new; but unfortunately what was true was not new, and what was new was not true."

In greater and smaller ways the Enlightenment presumption is still common in many modern references to time. All too often there is a double presumption at work. On the one hand, the present is privileged over the past. On the other hand, the future is privileged over the present. The meaning of the term modern is "just now," but presumption comes in when belief in what is "just now" becomes inflated into a "constitutional claim for nowness as newness." Philosopher Martin Heidegger attacks the presumption in the way we view the present as "the proudly Exclusive Now" or, worse still, as "the strutting point."

Paradox

The third deeper consequence of our modern view of time is *paradox*. Such is the speed and pressure of time in our world that incessant change plays havoc with our categories and our conclusions. Settled convictions, assured judgments, long-held beliefs, age-old traditions, newly trumpeted discoveries, and radical new fashions are all swept away without ceremony in the tornado of change that is modern time. Little wonder that in sphere after sphere we face a harvest of ironies and unintended consequences. Or that many of our categories, such as left/right and liberal/conservative, have become so tattered, confusing, and outworn.

In 1939, the midnight hour of the twentieth century when Hitler and Stalin stunned the world with news of their Nazi-Soviet Pact, an English wag remarked that "All our Isms are Wasms." His point is even more apt today. Popular categories have been worn out by overuse and distorted beyond recognition by the unsparing speed of time. How else can one explain what we sometimes see of the amiable hollowness of traditionalism, the blind illiberalism of liberalism, or the breathless progressivism of conservatism?

"The avant-garde is the rear guard" is said today with good reason, for many twenty-first–century liberals have eighteenth-century views of progress, nineteenth-century views of science, and mid-twentieth–century views of facts and objectivity. The problem is not that these positions are dated—the error of chronological snobbery is itself is a legacy of modern time—but that they are untrue.

The paradox is evident on the conservative side too. Many conservatives, it is said, hate liberals more than they love freedom. But that is only the beginning of the contortions. Above all, conservatives today are anything but conservative when it comes to business and the environment. In these areas no one could be more stridently progressive than our brave conservatives. Historian John Lukacs writes, " 'Conservatives,' especially in the United States, are some of the most strident proponents of 'Progress'; their views of the present and future are not merely shortsighted but laden with a bellowing optimism that is imbecile rather than naive."

These ironies lead us right back to our central concern—how an unprecedented Christian pursuit of relevance has led directly to an unprecedented Christian irrelevance. To this special problem we can now turn, with this vivid awareness of how the pressures of modern time shape all our lives, including our life of faith.

PART TWO

SHORN OF OUR SECRET STRENGTH

THREE

IMPOSSIBLE STANCES

A VITAL SECRET OF THE CHURCH'S POWER AND GLORY in history lies in its calling to be "against the world, for the world." C. S. Lewis calls this the "two-edged character" of the Christian faith. Based on the twin truths of creation and the fall, Christians see everything with a bifocal vision—they view reality not only in terms of what the world was created to be but also of what it has come to be. As a result, the Christian faith is simultaneously both world-affirming and world-denying.

When the church is weak or careless in maintaining this dual stance, it leads directly to cowardice and corruption, decadence and decline. But when the church is faithful, it lies at the core of her power to transform and renew culture. As the long and distinguished story of Christian reformers shows, followers of Jesus support the best in human aspirations and achievements while resisting the worst.

Unlike Eastern religions, such as Hinduism and Buddhism, the Christian faith is unashamedly world-affirming. "All truth is God's truth," so the best of the good, the true, and the beautiful can be supported wherever it is to be found. The church therefore has a glorious record of creativity in art, music, and literature; in founding schools and colleges; in running hospitals and orphanages; in caring for the poor and oppressed; and in pursuing reforms and advancing human rights.

At the same time, the Christian faith, unlike the secular varieties of humanism, is also world-denying. Whatever law or practice contradicts God's law or principles must be confronted. The church therefore emphasizes reforms as well as maintenance, calls for fasts as well as feasts, stresses self-denial as well as fulfillment, and has at its heart the scandal of the cross as well as the hope of glory. Along with Judaism, the Christian faith is neither one thing nor the other but emphatically both at once. This is a vital secret of its strength.

Jesus called his followers to be "in" the world but "not of" the world, but only he accomplished it perfectly.

But there is a simple snag with this powerful stance: It is easier said than done. It was Jesus himself who called his followers to be "in" the world but "not of" the world, and so to be "against the world for the world." But only he accomplished it perfectly. As the two-thousand–year history of the church shows, it is much easier to go to one extreme or the other. Either we are so much "in" the world that we are "of it," or we are so much "not of" the world that we are "other-worldly" and, as the jibe goes, of "no earthly use."

Starkly clear examples illustrate when people and periods have gone to the extremes. The Renaissance papacy in the fifteenth century, for instance, was unrivaled in its worldly pursuit of secular power and its brazen embrace of evil; the Borgia popes such as Alexander VI led the hall of shame in their corruption, adultery, murder, and incest.

But the long, mixed record also teaches two important lessons: One concerns the typical stances we are likely to take in engaging the world; the other concerns the fact that the modern world—including its attitudes toward time—makes all of the stances harder than ever.

In short, of all the cultures the church has lived in, the modern world is the most powerful, the most pervasive, and the most pressurizing. And it has done more damage to Christian integrity and effectiveness than all the persecutors of the church in history.

This is why we must not take false comfort from the church's extraordinary growth in the South. The exploding churches in Asia, Africa, and Latin America are largely premodern. What is happening there is truly astonishing, but these churches have not gone through the fiery trial of modernity that has devastated the church in Europe and has destroyed faith among leaders and thinking people in the United States.

Of all the cultures the church has lived in, the modern world is the most powerful, the most pervasive, and the most pressurizing.

But for our purposes here, the significance of the modern world is straightforward. Each of the three traditional stances that Christians can take toward the world has been made immeasurably harder. As we shall see as we examine them, the pressures and temptations at the heart of the modern world are behind the difficulties in each case.

Defiance Is Untenable

The first traditional stance of Christians toward the world is, to use sociologist Peter Berger's helpful categories, that of *cognitive and cultural resistance.* Taking seriously the biblical warning to "flee the world," this first stance is founded on a realistic assessment of the dangers of the world and of worldliness. It then channels this awareness into a determined resistance to the spirit and system of the world of its day. The long history of monasticism is the most distinguished example of this stance, but expressions of world-denying communities, such as the Amish and the Mennonites, are still evident today.

What is critical, however, is that the modern world has rendered this stance largely impotent and almost non-existent. Such is the power, pervasiveness, and attractiveness of the modern world—in a word, its lure—that few Christians are willing to think or live decisively "not of" it. A genuine world-denying stance today is rare.

I can well remember the occasion when this point came home to me for the first time. My tutor at Oxford, an eminent European scholar, raised a question at a crowded social sciences seminar in the mid-seventies. "By the end of the 1970s," he asked, "who will be the worldliest Christians in America?" There was an audible gasp when he eventually answered his own query: "I guarantee it will be the evangelicals and fundamentalists."

But surely, people were thinking, evangelicals and fundamentalist were world-denying *by definition.* Defying the world was central to their convictions and a salient part of their profile. True, the professor argued, they once were like that. The traditional evangelical and fundamentalist had a fear of secular culture and a legendary nose for the "worldly" that was worthy of a blood hound or a Geiger counter.

For example, on my first visit to the United States in 1968, I was speaking at a church in the South and made a passing reference to an Ingmar Bergman film. I was roundly booed. Christians in that part of the world, I was told, did not go to films. Nor apparently did they drink wine or think that Jesus drank wine—and I was left in no uncertainty that my Irish brewing background was highly suspect, to say the least.

Not long after that, a friend of mine who is now an eminent and nationally known journalist was told by a seminary professor, "If you go to work in the secular media, no Christian man will ever want to marry you. And you'll lose your faith!"

Evangelicals and fundamentalists have embraced the modern world with a passion unrivaled in history.

The years since the prediction at that Oxford seminar have shown beyond question that evangelicals and fundamentalists have embraced the modern world with a passion unrivaled in history. Again, let no one misunderstand. I do not write as a detached or unsympathetic observer. I am an evangelical, a deeply convinced and unashamed evangelical—one who, together with all those from whatever Christian tradition, define themselves and their lives by the first things of the gospel of Jesus Christ.

But the blunt, sad fact is that we evangelicals, in the most prominent form of the evangelical community or subculture, are becoming the strongest rival to mainline Protestantism as the worldliest Christian tradition in America. From a general materialism and secularity in priorities and preoccupations, to particular captivities to such modern idols as psychology, management, and marketing, the pattern is starkly plain.

The faith-world of John Wesley, Jonathan Edwards, John Jay, William Wilberforce, Hannah More, Lord Shaftesbury, Catherine Booth, Hudson Taylor, D. L. Moody, Charles Spurgeon, Oswald Chambers, Andrew Murray, Carl Henry, and John Stott is disappearing. In its place a new evangelicalism is arriving in which therapeutic self-concern overshadows knowing God, spirituality displaces theology, end-times escapism crowds out day-to-day discipleship, marketing triumphs over mission, references to opinion polls outweigh reliance on biblical exposition, concerns for power and relevance are more obvious than concern for piety and faithfulness, talk of reinventing the church has replaced prayer for revival, and the characteristic evangelical passion for missionary enterprise is overpowered by the all-consuming drive to sustain the multiple business empires of the booming evangelical subculture.

Many evangelicals are blind to the sea change because they know only the present and have little sense of history, even their own. Where there is a vague awareness that the old views of worldliness have gone, it is characteristically covered by resorting to the "fallacy of the fear." That is, a fear of one extreme is cited to excuse the collapse into another. "Thank God," our new evangelicals say, "that we have escaped from the 'do's and don'ts' and 'no-nos' of the narrow worldliness of the previous generation. Our forefathers were hidebound and legalists. They majored in the minors and reduced worldliness to drinking, dancing, and smoking. Let's escape from such restrictive worldliness and celebrate grace and our Christian freedom."

The fear, of course, is legitimate. The dead hand of legalism is the antithesis of the gospel and grace. But the fallacy comes in when true worldliness is thrown out with trivialized worldliness. Any determined effort to resist the world will certainly entail pitfalls and dangers, and they need to be understood and resisted. But they are not the urgent danger of today, which for the moment is predominantly on the other side.

Negotiation Is Challenging

The second traditional stance of Christians toward the world is that of *cognitive and cultural negotiation*. Taking seriously the biblical admonition to be "not conformed to the world, but transformed by the renewing of the mind," this stance is the middle one of the three. It seeks to maintain an ongoing practice of discerning between true and false, good and bad, the godly and the worldly.

This stance can be covered quickly, for there is no principled problem inherent in it today. Indeed, the greatest thinkers, such as St. Augustine, have exemplified it clearly. And almost all Christians would say they follow it, whatever positions they may end up with in reality.

But there is a very practical problem in pursuing this stance today: The modern world makes it harder than ever. Such is the scale and speed of the information and the issues we currently confront that our powers of discernment and discrimination are taxed to exhaustion. Which of us can read enough, think enough, and pray enough to be wise enough? There is simply too much to take in and to ponder.

Thinking and acting Christianly in the blizzard of modern information and change requires the courage of a prophet, the wisdom of a sage, and the character of a saint—not to speak of the patience of Job and the longevity of Methuselah.

Thinking and acting Christianly in the blizzard of modern information and change requires the courage of a prophet, the wisdom of a sage, and the character of a saint.

Adaptation Is Unfaithful

The third traditional stance of Christians toward the world is the one most distorted by the pressures of modern time. This is the stance of *cognitive and cultural adaptation*. It takes seriously the biblical call to mission, and in particular the pattern of the incarnation and the example of the Apostle Paul of being "a Jew to the Jews, a gentile to the gentiles, and all things to all people." In doing so this stance seeks to adapt the gospel creatively to every new people and culture so as to be relevant to the world of its day.

The impulse behind this third stance is admirable. It is unquestionably correct and worthy, a passion that should be evident in all followers of Jesus Christ. If the first stance emphasizes the church's faithfulness, this one emphasizes her flexibility. The church of Christ is "a community for others" rather than for itself, which means that service always entails adaptability.

But there is a huge pitfall when this stance is pushed to the limit. And the central force of the modern world is to ensure that it always goes to an extreme. For the end of the line in adopting a mode of uncritical adaptation is a reaching out for relevance that ends up toppling over into surrender to the modern world, therefore becoming unfaithful to Christ.

How does this collapse into worldliness happen? Both the process and the problems it creates can be spelled out clearly. A stance that starts out commendably with a passion for relevance moves through four steps to end disastrously in unfaithfulness and irrelevance. Let's examine each of the steps below.

Step One: Assumption

The process of uncritical adaptation begins when some aspect of modern thought or life is assumed either to be significant, and therefore worth acknowledging, or superior to what Christians know or do, and therefore worth adopting. Soon the assumption in question becomes an integral part of Christian thought and practice. Since all truth is God's truth, there is an immediate plausibility to this idea.

The danger comes, however, when an assumption is accepted without any thought—simply because it is modern. For instance, modern capitalism is clearly the most powerful engine in all history for creating wealth, but that does not mean that we should adopt all the principles of market capitalism without critiquing them. Assumptions about anything, whether capitalism, science, politics, psychology, patriotism, fast food, or the place of celebrities in modern society, should all be recognized and carefully examined.

Step Two: Abandonment

Everything that does not fit in with the new assumption (made in step one) either is cut out deliberately or is slowly relegated to a limbo of neglect. This change is far more than tactical or temporary, on the order of a golfer choosing a particular club for a specific shot. Playing from a bunker or in the rough, he may pick out an iron rather than a driver or a putter, but he will still have all his clubs in his golf bag and the next hole may require a club not used at the previous hole.

What happens in this step is more drastic. Truths or customs that do not fit in with the modern assumption are put up in the creedal attic to collect dust. They are of no more use. The modification or removal of offending assumptions is permanent. What begins as question of tactics escalates to a question of truth; apparently, the modern assumptions are authoritative. Is the traditional idea unfashionable, superfluous, or just plain wrong? No matter. It doesn't fit in, so it has to go.

In the arena of faith, the modern phase of this trend began in the eighteenth century, but the liberal heyday for abandoning tradition was the 1960s. Suddenly the new awareness of secularity, secularization, and the secular city made transcendence embarrassing and immanence all-important.

With this realization it was time to abandon old images and replace former practices, each one buried in its regulation shroud of caricature. God, they said, was not "a grandfather in the sky" but "the ground of being." Prayer was not a matter of "celestial shopping lists" but of meditation. Supernatural phenomena such as miracles were unintelligible to "users of radio and electricity." They needed to be "demythologized." With the exception of left-wing prophets thundering against the Establishment and the Vietnam War, "Thus saith the Lord" was replaced by the trademark saying of modern liberalism: "It is no longer possible to believe . . ."

The new evangelicals were in the process of becoming the old liberals.

In the 1980s and 1990s, it was the evangelical turn. Regardless of the fact that Protestant liberalism had chased every idea with skirts and lost its character, credibility, and national authority in the process, evangelicals set off on the same promiscuous spree. Suddenly the air in evangelical conferences and magazines was thick with assaults on the irrelevance of history, the outdatedness of traditional hymns and music, the uptightness of traditional moralism, the abstractness of theologizing, the impracticality of biblical exposition, the inadequacy of small churches, and the deadly, new unforgivable sin— irrelevance.

What had happened? The new evangelicals were in the process of becoming the old liberals. Church growth was now to be "on new grounds." Modern assumptions from the spheres of management, marketing, and psychology had become accepted without challenge.

The irony was underscored when chastened liberals began to point out with sadness that evangelicals were now making the same mistakes they had made earlier. Evangelical pastors, for instance, were criticized for being "shrinks in their pulpits and CEOs in their offices," which had been the critique of liberals in the 1960s. In other words, in swapping psychology for theology in their preaching and enthroning management and marketing in their church administration, evangelicals were making the same errors as liberals had earlier. Whatever the newly sharpened statements about biblical authority, the real authority of the Bible had been eclipsed in practice by the assumptions of the modern world.

Step Three: Adaptation

The third step follows logically from the second, just as the second does from the first. Something new is assumed; something old is abandoned; and everything else is adapted. In other words, what remains of traditional beliefs and practices is altered to fit with the new assumption. After all, the new assumption has become authoritative. It has entered the mind like a new boss at work, and everything must smartly change to suit its preferences and perspectives. What is not abandoned does not stay the same; rather, it is adapted.

The list of such recent Christian adaptations is lengthy—from Christian Marxism on the left-wing liberal side to Christian marketing on the conservative evangelical side. And the estimates of its success would vary too. For as with the second step, this third step cannot be faulted logically or theologically when considered on its own. Adaptability is a requirement of all cross-cultural translation, and the Christian faith throughout its history has shown an unrivaled genius for adaptability with faithfulness.

To be sure, Christian history is full of examples of constructive adaptation. In the nineteenth century, for instance, Hudson Taylor founded the China Inland Mission and scandalized Europeans when he took the gospel right into the interior of China, not just to the treaty ports where other Westerners stopped. Taking the incarnation as their pattern, and without ever compromising the gospel, he and his fellow-missionaries set out to become as Chinese as they could. In the process, they learned not just Mandarin but also local Chinese dialects, wore Chinese dress rather than Western, and adopted Chinese customs whenever appropriate. One of my favorite photos is of my grandfather, a doctor who treated the Imperial family as well as the poor, dressed sedately in his Mandarin-style gown and wearing Chinese pigtails.

The trouble with this step comes when Christians go further still—when the habits and assumptions of any age and culture are accepted without thought, and then replace the authority of traditional Christian assumptions. And this, in turn, leads to the fourth and final step.

Step Four: Assimilation

The fourth step is the logical culmination of the first three. Something modern is assumed (step one). As a consequence, something traditional is abandoned (step two), and everything else is adapted (step three). The outcome is that what remains is not only adapted but absorbed by the modern assumptions. It is assimilated without any decisive remainder. The result is worldliness, or Christian capitulation to some aspect of the culture of its day. No longer a missionary, the church "goes native" in some foreign culture or among some foreign ideas.

There are two main forms of assimilation. One is assimilation to modern ideas, which is best illustrated by Protestant liberalism. From Friedrich Schleiermacher in the eighteenth century, with his laudable mission to reach "the cultured despisers of the gospel," down to contemporary U.S. Episcopal bishops, with their brazen abandonment of Christian orthodoxy under a call for "a new Christianity for a new world," the development is clear. So also is the outcome—the incubation of worldliness, heresy, and even paganism among those who still call themselves leaders of the church but who believe little or nothing in common with the orthodox church of the last twenty centuries.

Without the decisive authority of the word of God that defined the true prophet, false prophets were simply captive to the culture they reflected.

In other words, the account of liberalism in its extremes is the story of constant transfers of allegiance, or of a starry-eyed series of affairs with the philosophical and cultural assumptions of its time. Understand the dominant thought of the day and you understand the infatuations of liberalism, for theology follows philosophy as a tail follows a dog. Eventually, as in the bizarre contortions of today's trendier church leaders, there is next-to-nothing of the Christian gospel and next-to-nothing-else but the modern philosophy—and this in the name of purported leaders of the Christian church and advocates of the Christian faith, latter day "false shepherds" if ever there were any.

Centuries ago the prophet Isaiah of Jerusalem charged that the false prophets of his day were "the tail" of Judah's society. They were not simply behind; they were behind because they were the tail that followed the dog. Without the decisive authority of the word of God that defined the true prophet, false prophets were simply captive to the culture they reflected. They were popular, they were entertaining, they were soothing, they were convenient, they were fashionable— and they were utterly false. In today's world, the stance of the wagging tail has been elevated to the level of a creed. In 1966, the World Council of Churches even adopted the bizarre dictum, "The world must set the agenda for the Church."

Many liberals would dispute this charge of assimilation indignantly, but the evidence is incontrovertible—above all in their own negative assessment of their own predecessors. What did they criticize? Their predecessors' uncritical adherence to the philosophical and cultural assumptions of their day. For example, the views of Jesus in the nineteenth-century church historian Adolf Harnack were dismissed famously in this way, "The Christ that Harnack sees . . . is only the reflection of a Liberal Protestant face at the bottom of a deep well." Albert Schweitzer's criticism of liberalism in the early twentieth century was the same. Modern theology "mixes history with everything and ends by being proud of the skill with which it finds its own thoughts."

The spectacle is poignant. Theology, former Queen of the Sciences, has lost her throne and is now earning her living as a runway model in the fashion houses of today's thought. Philosophies come and go as fashions do, usually with the best European houses determining each season's new lines. Liberalism's hapless task is to copy and mass produce the mistress's new lines slavishly. Many of the secular proponents of today's wilder expressions of paganism, liberated sexuality, and gender politics could answer the extremes of Protestant liberalism with the famous quip of Oscar Wilde: "I not only follow you. I precede you."

So as we've seen, the first form of assimilation is to modern ideas. And as we will explore below, the other is to modern practices. The last generation of evangelicals provides clear examples of this. The air is abuzz with the future. The "coming church" and the "emerging church" are everything. The talk is all of new ways of "doing church" through reinventing, revising, innovating, borrowing, mixing, and experimenting. Everything now has to be "intentional" and "on-purpose." Ministers are no longer theological authorities but the "chief story-tellers" and "facilitators of a joint spiritual journey." "Dysfunctional churches" that are not "attuned to the world" are "reinvented for the present age" in a myriad of "intentional" ways, all with their "value propositions" clearly specified and their "measurable outcomes" clarified in advance. Music and worship services are designed for audiences as if congregations were "specialized niches on music sales charts" or the newly discovered fruit of demographic research.

But where in all this movement is the prayer to match the punditry? Is the church ours to reinvent, or is it God's? Does the head of the church have anything to say, or do the consultants have the last word? Shouldn't "doing church" follow from what we believe is the church's being? Was the church first invented by a previous generation, so that it is our job to do it again, or is the church's real need for the revival and reformation that can only come from God?

Some have spent the last decades reinventing churches furiously according to the dictates of the baby boomers. Others are now pronouncing that passé and are tackling the task with the same enthusiasm to court the younger generation. But what links them all is the same principle. The authentic church is the relevant church, and the relevant church is the attuned church, and the attuned church is the church in sync with its audience.

> *A great part of the evangelical community has transferred authority from* **Sola Scriptura** *to* **Sola Cultura.**

Will our brave new evangelicals be able to change ships nimbly on every falling tide? Or will their efforts degenerate into a culture of betrayal as much as liberalism did earlier? There are signs pointing to the latter, particularly in the growing casualness about bad theology. But there are also alarm bells ringing at the more dismal examples of evangelical worldliness, such as the incidence of nepotism among leaders and pornography among pastors. For the moment, however, an overall trend is plain. For all the lofty recent statements on biblical authority, a great part of the evangelical community has made a historic shift. It has transferred authority from *Sola Scriptura* (by Scripture alone) to *Sola Cultura* (by culture alone).

Is the culture decisive and the audience sovereign for the Christian church? Not for one moment. God forbid. The client and the consumer may be king for free-market enterprise. Serving the shareholders may be obligatory for the directors of corporations. But the church of Christ is not under the sway of market totalitarianism—even in America where capitalism is king, pope, and emperor all rolled into one. From the prophets' "This is the word of the Lord" to the reformer's "Here I stand; so help me, God, I can do no other," the message, not the audience, is always sovereign, and the culture is always potentially the world set over against Christ and his kingdom. To think and live otherwise is to recycle the classic error of liberalism and to court the worldliness, irrelevance, and spiritual adultery that it represents.

Is the culture decisive and the audience sovereign for the Christian church? Not for one moment.

Have we wrestled seriously with the theological and historical significance of these misguided approaches? Have we learned the salutary lesson from the story of the self-inflicted wounds of Protestant liberalism? *It is not too much to say that the combined efforts of such Protestant liberal renegades and revisionists are a key part of the story of the loss of the West by the Christian church. More importantly, such ex-believers, who put other gods* before *God, and weakly believing re-interpreters, who put other gods* beside *God, are the main reason for the loss of the Christian gospel in much of the Christian church in the West today.*

For as the reinterpretations deepen, the losses steadily mount:

First, there is a loss of courage. The reinterpretations are always in one direction only.

Second, there is a loss of continuity. The diluted faith is no longer the faith of our fathers and mothers, handed down to us across the generations; it is a different faith.

Third, there is a loss of credibility. There is too little of believable substance that any thoughtful person is asked to believe.

And finally, there is a loss of identity. As a celebrated atheist philosopher said of the watered-down liberalism of his day, "At that point the creed becomes a way of saying what the infidel next door believes too."

In the stinging rebuke of the nineteenth-century Danish philosopher Søren Kierkegaard, such faithless believers are "kissing Judases"—those who pretend to embrace Jesus even as they betray him.

FOUR

SIREN CALLS
TO CAPTIVITY

IN THE 1930S, as the European democracies drifted weakly toward war, Winston Churchill used to quote Alexander the Great to sound the alarm. "The Persians would always be slaves," Alexander said, "because they did not know how to pronounce the word No." Independent thinking, protest, refusal, resistance, and the courage to say *no* are all essential to the vigilance that sees something is wrong and is willing to stand up and take action. But what we often forget is the long, slow process that is entailed for these qualities to gain their fighting trim as attitudes of resistance.

That was certainly so with the resistance in wartime France. When Colonel (later General, later President) Charles de Gaulle issued his famous four-minute rallying cry on behalf of the "free French" from the BBC in London in July 1940, there was no resistance movement waiting to spring into action at his words. Humiliated, compromised, and demoralized by the speed and ferocity of their capitulation to the Nazi invasion, the French people were in no condition for heroism. The great slogans of the Third Republic—Liberté, Fraternité, Egalité—were discredited, but nothing had taken their place. The word "Degaulliste," used of the supporters of De Gaulle, was virtually the equivalent of "disloyal." "Patrie" (the fatherland) was as much used by the left-wing to speak of international communism as it was to speak of France.

The nearest idea to resistance was the rare, early talk of mounting some sort of "refusal" to the Germans and the even rarer talk of creating a "secret army." In short, the road to the heroism and daring of the powerful, later French resistance movement and the Maquis underground was long, tortuous, and uneven.

Across the West as a whole, there is little apparent appetite for a long, sustained struggle with the challenges of the modern world.

The same is true of reform in the church today. Across the West as a whole, there is little apparent appetite for a long, sustained struggle with the challenges of the modern world. With rare pockets of exception, the European church has capitulated to the triumph of the modern world much as the French did to the Nazis, and with the same resulting demoralization and divisions.

The same is true in the United States of many of the church's intelligentsia. It has been decades since they thought seriously of a sustained and decisive response to the modern world that was decisively Christian. As we saw in the last chapter, mimicking modernity in Christian language is the best that many Christian thinkers have been able to muster for some time.

And what of the heartlands of the faith at the popular level, where the numbers are still astonishing, the dedication still powerful, and the wealth and ingenuity still undimmed? Alas, the story there is of myopia. Many are complacent in their privatized faith and their prosperous subcultures or are unaware that the tools they are using to remedy their irrelevance are actually making it worse.

The crying need of the Western church today is for reformation and revival, and for a decisive liberation from the Babylonian captivity of modernity. In other words, what followers of Jesus need is the freedom from the forces of the modern world that prevent independent thinking and living with integrity. Our deepest necessity is to be shaped by our faith rather than by the pushes and pulls of the world.

This short book is only about one aspect of that captivity—*to the pressures of the modern view of time.* But this element is part and parcel of the overall captivity of the modern world, and it is worth noting how it fits in with the other aspects.

> *The crying need of the Western church today is for reformation and revival.*

In particular, we must resist three forces of cultural captivity today. Closely related and overlapping, they form a large part of the Babylonian captivity from which we Christians in the modern world must be freed. The third force, which grows from the heart of our modern view of time, is the particular focus of this book, but all require resisting.

The Lure of Others

The first siren call toward cultural captivity is *conformity,* the power of the pull of others. Always a danger in human thinking, the lure of conformity to others' ideas and practices is greatly increased in the age of democracy. As Alexis de Tocqueville warned in *Democracy in America* in 1835, the temper of democratic times could lead as easily to the tyranny of the majority as to rampant individualism.

When this happens, as Orestes Brownson pointed out in the same period, we make the mistake of replacing the divine right of kings with the equally mistaken divine right of the people. For public opinion as the voice of the people is no more infallible than the voice of kings, presidents, or religious leaders. None are sacrosanct and all require challenging. But for us the power of public opinion is the most dangerous because it is today's danger.

Whereas our grandparents lived as if they had swallowed gyroscopes, we think and act as if we have swallowed Gallup polls.

Warnings such as these are needed now more than ever. We have shifted, it is said, from an "inner-directed" society to an "other-directed" society. Such is the power of our peers, the media, opinion surveys, focus groups, and the demographic accuracy of marketing. Our opinions and our ethics all too easily become a matter of consensus that are shaped by our awareness of others rather than by a compass planted in us by our parents, our upbringing, and our own conscious convictions.

Whereas our grandfathers and grandmothers lived as if they had swallowed gyroscopes, we think and act as if we have swallowed

Gallup polls. Our thinking is all too easily "group thinking"—that which is shaped by a desire for concurrence rather than by critical thought.

In the secular world, the climax of these trends was the emergence of "political correctness." For when truth's importance decays, independent thinking, debate, and disagreements decay too. Then, just as iron filings are naturally attracted to the most powerful magnet, popular opinion naturally gravitates to the most powerful and fashionable views in the room. The result is political correctness, or abject conformity to powerful, fashionable opinion.

But we who are people of faith should not cast stones. There are forms of "theological correctness" in the church that are really only current opinion that has been inflated with the mantle of theological authority. And this "TC movement" is far from truly correct theologically.

Conformity, of course, is not necessarily bad. It all depends what we are conforming to. A closely related term to conformity is respectability. Thus *morality* (the practice of virtue because we know it is right) is preferable to *respectability* (the practice of virtue because we are seen). But respectability in turn is preferable to *hypocrisy* (the practice of virtue because we are afraid of being seen to be bad), just as hypocrisy is preferable to *wickedness* (the complete abandonment of any pretense to virtue of any kind).

It was in this sense that La Rochefoucauld, the seventeenth-century French writer who was the author of celebrated maxims, observed that hypocrisy is the homage that vice pays to virtue. But while hypocrisy is preferable to wickedness, and respectability to hypocrisy, genuine virtue is the best of all.

Independent thinking, of course, is a key part of genuine virtue. In fact, independent thinking is what prevents the corruption of concurrence-thinking from collapsing into conformity, and thus stops the slide from respectability to hypocrisy to wickedness.

The Power of Approval

The second siren call toward cultural captivity is *popularity*, the power of the pull of approval. This form of captivity is closely related to the first, with other factors reinforcing those at work in the pull toward conformity. Again take the molding power of the temper of democracy. Abraham Lincoln's government "of the people, by the people, for the people" is obviously the idealized view of democracy, just as Alexis de Tocqueville's "tyranny of the majority" is its corrupt form.

John Lukacs has described our position today as moving from the danger of the tyranny of the majority to the equal danger of the rule of the minority in the name of the majority: "What counts is what people want"/ "People don't know what they want"/ "Experts know what people want"/ "People are told what they want"/ "People want what they are told."

The power of popularity and approval are strong forces in this development, so much so that democratic elections have increasingly become popularity contests and, worse still, publicity contests. All that we examined about the lure of conformity comes in here again, but there are other factors at work too. For instance, one is the triumph of the therapeutic revolution and its emphasis on self-esteem that so easily becomes a voracious hunger for approval.

Another is the emergence of identity politics and its focus on group status with its attendant craving for approval.

We all like to be liked. We all want to be thought well of. We all prefer approval to disapproval.

In such a climate, we all like to be liked. We all want to be thought well of. We all prefer approval to disapproval. We all feel entitled to be recognized and treated as we think we deserve, and we all live to maximize the chances of that happening.

The desire for approval, then, is a major driving force in modern society. From our consumer choices to our expressions of opinion to our selection of mates and faiths, a lust for approval is never far from our thinking and our actions as modern people. And instead of looking for approval to the one audience, the Audience of One, we look for it in the shifting sands of public opinion.

The Seduction of Timeliness

The third siren call toward cultural captivity is *fashionability*, the power of the pull of corrupt timeliness or distorted relevance. As I stressed in the introduction, relevance is not the problem but rather a distorted relevance that slips into trendiness, triviality, and transience. Here the lure of our modern sense of time is most powerful and damaging.

Future Madness

The nineteenth century was a century of astonishing change. It may even have experienced the greatest and most significant changes in all human history, outstripping even the twentieth century. But whereas the major nineteenth-century response was, in Tennyson's phrase, "the passion of the past," the twentieth-century response to change has been what novelist Milan Kundera has called "the fascination with the future."

Our current passion for the future has been called future fixation, or future madness. For those caught up in this frenzy, the past is dry, dusty, and remote, an albatross around our necks. By contrast, the future rushes toward us gleaming and bright, breathlessly desirable and technologically as alluring as it is inevitable.

"The future is history," we are told with the gushing enthusiasm of the PR junkie. "Tomorrow just happened." "Join us or be left behind." With slogans like these expressing the mentality of the times, Lukacs comments dryly that our supreme purpose as humans is to be "reception committees" to welcome the purported glories of the coming future.

The Christian church has been taken over by this frenzy as deeply as anyone. The past is seen as beside the point, outdated, reactionary, stagnant. In a word that is today's supreme term of dismissal, the past is irrelevant. Everything Christian from worship to evangelism must be fresh, new, up-to-date, attuned, appealing, seeker-sensitive, audience-friendly, and relentlessly relevant, relevant, relevant. "All-new," "must-read," "the sequel that is more than equal"—the mentality is rampant and the effects are corrosive.

Results of Pursuing Relevance

What are some of the effects of our unthinking pursuit of relevance? Let's look at five.

First, much Christian pursuit of timeliness has become trivial. Following trends passionately but promiscuously, many Christian leaders have become trendy. Obsessed with the new, they have produced only novelty. Staggering from one high of excitement to another, they have become jaded.

Evangelicals were once known as "the serious people." It is sad to note that today many evangelicals are the most superficial of religious believers—lightweight in thinking, gossamer-thin in theology, and avid proponents of spirituality-lite in terms of preaching and responses to life. What started out as breathless and excited is ending as exhausted and out-of-breath.

> *Evangelicals were once known as "the serious people."*

Second, in the pursuit of timeliness some Christian spokespersons have become deceptive—or at least have promised far more than they have delivered. As George Orwell said, futurism is "the major mental disease of our time." A quack science, it picks up current trends, projects them into the future, and then pretends that the results are predictions. Futurist John Naisbitt was therefore correct as well as candid when he admitted that he was really a "Nowist" rather than a futurist or a prophet. Would that the new breed of "pastor-futurists" were as honest.

Third, the recent Christian pursuit of relevance has all too often led to transience. In the late nineteenth century, Nietzsche scornfully dismissed the German writer David Strauss: "He has succeeded in becoming famous for a couple of hours in our times." Thus Nietzsche long predated Andy Warhol's comment on people being famous for fifteen minutes. He realized that with our modern obsession with change, the traditional human perspective of "under the aspect of eternity" *(sub specie aeternitatis)* had become "under the aspect of two hours."

The endless pursuit of relevance leads only to transience and burn-out. Many years ago, Dean Inge of St. Paul's Cathedral in London remarked, in words that could be the epitaph for many trendy church leaders, "He who marries the spirit of the age soon becomes a widower." As with great art, faith that lasts is faith that answers to standards higher than today's trends.

"He who marries the spirit of the age soon becomes a widower."
— *Dean Inge*

Fourth, the Christian pursuit of relevance is so commercially profitable in the short term that we would be wise to look out for the salesman's agenda and his bottom line. "Prepare to meet the future or be overrun by it!" we are told by countless hawkers of seminars. In other words, in a world of experts, specialists, and consultants, pundits have become the prime ideas-mongers and secular prophets of our day. Once they achieve celebrity, they pronounce on all subjects and are quoted on all occasions.

A superior class of pundit might even be called "pan-pundits"—intellectuals who have the ability to talk about anything and everything without a corresponding knowledge or humility. Sign on to learn from one or another and you will gain the secrets of the world over the horizon, have the edge over all your competitors, and know how to face the future with confidence and the best insights that money can buy. In a word, you will be future-savvy and well able to meet what comes with all the self-assurance of an in-touch, information-proficient relevant leader.

Forgive me, but has no one noticed that trendspotting itself has become a trend? And that as trendspotters tell our fortunes, they make theirs? As one philosopher puts it bluntly, addressing our vulnerability to experts and consultants in an age of future-mania, "The so-called Future, with a capital F, is actually no one's fate but someone's present plan with which the rest are bidden to go along."

Fifth, and finally, the recent Christian obsession with relevance and the future leads all too often to moral and intellectual cowardice. Afraid to challenge the power of progress and the lure of the latest, or to delay the arrival of the brave, new future, we bite our lips and cave in weakly to what we know in our hearts is neither right, nor wise, nor lasting. As the French writer Charles Peguy wrote a century ago, "It will never be known what acts of cowardice have been motivated by the fear of not looking sufficiently progressive."

Like the other siren calls to captivity, the lure of fashionability is as abject as it is effortless unless we are prepared to resist and be on our guard. We turn next, in part 3, to not only the cost but the real benefits of faithfulness.

PART THREE

RESTORING THE ARCHIMEDEAN POINT

FIVE

THE PRICE OF
FAITHFULNESS

A FRENCH RESISTANCE LEADER was once asked how he explained the fact that his men had been so heroic. He thought for a while, and then answered: "We weren't heroic. We were simply maladjusted enough to know that something was seriously wrong." Seen one way, his reply reveals the perspective that led to the courage for them to break with their own people and take on the Nazis. Seen another way, it also reveals the pain that lay behind the stance. But the perspective and the pain are linked; the position that gives the benefit of the perspective is the same position that brings the burden of the pain.

This tough lesson is unmistakable in the saga of the unheeded messengers that haunt the pages of history. Two of the most famous—Jeremiah and John the Baptist—have left their hallmark on the very genre of public warnings. Every time we speak of a "jeremiad" we tip our caps to the weeping prophet, and we pay a belated compliment to the wild man of Judea every time we talk of "a voice crying in the wilderness."

But our modern use of these expressions also underscores why these messengers went unheeded. The jeremiad has become the art form of denunciation and lament—so much so that to use the word is virtually to dismiss the claim. It's only a "jeremiad," we say. "Things aren't what they used to be, but what's new?" "Another grumpy old man has harrumphed, but what are old men for?" The one thing no one actually needs to do is take the warning seriously.

To be sure, there is sometimes a grudging respect when we refer to someone as "a voice crying in the wilderness." But the phrase is used positively mostly in hindsight, and it is employed as often when referring to those best left in the wilderness. That is, those considered uncouth, annoying, and not worth heeding.

In our own generation the figure of the unheeded messenger was well represented by Alexander Solzhenitsyn in 1978 with his warning to the West in his Harvard commencement speech, "A World Split Apart." The years since he spoke have amply justified his highlighting of such problems as "the tilt of freedom toward evil," but the man who was lionized for his stand against communism was not appreciated for his stand against liberalism.

But unquestionably, the twentieth century's greatest example was Winston Churchill during his "wilderness years" in the 1930s, when his insistent warnings about the mounting menace of Hitler left him out of the government and out of favor with much of public opinion. Far-sighted, alone, somber, and indefatigable, he was appalled by what he called the "mush, slush, and gush" of a pacifist-dreaming Britain, a corrupt and divided France, and a remote and indifferent America. All of them were being led or lulled into oblivion before the menace of the rapidly rearming Nazis.

In 1936, when the Stanley Baldwin government called for a review of the situation, Churchill commented acidly,

> Anyone can see what the situation is. The Government simply cannot make up their mind, or they cannot get the Prime Minister to make up his mind. So they go on in a strange paradox, decided only to be

undecided, resolved to be irresolute, adamant for drift,
solid for fluidity, all powerful to be impotent.

The sleepwalking democracies with "leaderless confusion" were
unwittingly preparing more years "for the locusts to eat." Or as
Churchill muttered at London's Savoy Hotel as he heard the sounds
of merriment from those celebrating the Munich agreement, "These
poor people! They little know what they will have to face."

History's unheeded messengers have varied widely in both outcome and temperament. Some lived to see their vindication; some
did not. Winston Churchill—aristocratic, cigar-chomping, and ebul-
lient—is a far cry from John the Baptist, who is traditionally seen
as wild-eyed and dining on locusts and wild honey. But despite such
differences, common virtues emerge: discernment of the times;
courage to repudiate powerful interests and fashion; perseverance in
the face of daunting odds; seasoned wisdom born of a sense of history
and their nation's place in it; and—supremely with the Hebrew
prophets—a note of authority in their message born of its transcendent source.

No feature of the unheeded messengers, however, is more common than the link between the brilliance of their perspective and
the burden of their pain. Would Amos have thundered so boldly if he
had been a northern guild-prophet rather than a southern sheep
farmer? Would John the Baptist have spoken as bluntly if he had
been a courtier in Herod's palace? Could Martin Luther have seen
the church's captivity as clearly if he had been a cardinal in Rome?
Would Winston Churchill have spoken as freely as a member of the
Cabinet as he did as a backbencher from Chartwell? Possibly; we
are free to speculate.

In the reality of history, however, there is a clear link between each messenger's perspective and each messenger's pain. Both are the result of their being outsiders, and for any Christians who would speak out today in a time of the church's deepening cultural captivity, prophetic untimeliness carries a clear cost. In fact, there are three in particular.

Misfits in an Ill-Fitting World

The first cost of prophetic untimeliness is *a sense of maladjustment.* When society is increasingly godless and the church increasingly corrupt, faithfulness carries a price: The man or woman who lives by faith does not fit in. When the resistance leader said his men were "maladjusted enough to know that something was seriously wrong," he was brushing away a compliment to explain his men's clear-sightedness. He could as easily have pointed the other way. His men were maladjusted enough to see through the Nazi's "night and fog" that had befuddled their fellow-citizens.

> *The man or woman who lives by faith*
> *does not fit in.*

But the resistance leader also meant simply that they were maladjusted. In the France of their day they were misfits, outsiders, oddballs, discordant, and out of step. To have been maladjusted in an age that itself is later seen to be out of joint may be a comfort in the light of history and eternity, but in one's own time it can be highly uncomfortable.

Being out of sync or out of step is always slightly disconcerting. After all, good communication requires timing and harmony. That is why the nineteenth-century French novelist Stendhal wrote, "Wit ought to be only two degrees above the public mind. If it is five or six degrees ahead, it gives them an intolerable headache." In that sense good humor is always local and often translates badly across different cultures. But what is true of puns and jokes is infinitely more so of delivering an unpopular message: A speaker whose message is out of sync with the audience can feel terribly awkward, while often annoying or angering the audience.

Of course, it is easy to find comfort after the event, and there are many noble sayings about those prepared to buck the trends of their day and march with Thoreau to "a different drummer." For instance, the Roman historian Livy gave the famous advice: "Never mind if they call your caution timidity, your wisdom sloth, your generalship weakness; it is better that a wise enemy fear you than that foolish friends should praise." Nietzsche upheld untimeliness in a similar manner: "If you want biographies, do not desire those which bear the legend 'Herr-So-and-So and his age' but those upon whose title page there would stand 'a fighter against his age.'"

In the same vein, C. S. Lewis referred to himself in his inaugural lecture at Cambridge as an "Old Western man," a "dinosaur," and a "Neanderthaler." In short, praised prophets are mostly dead prophets, though in their lifetimes they were skunks in the parfumerie or heretics in the revival meeting.

All that is true, but it is important to add that, though faithfulness may entail maladjustment, maladjustment does not necessarily indicate faithfulness; we may just be odd and using maladjustment to rationalize our oddness. But the point still holds: The pain of maladjustment arising from faithfulness may still be intense. There is no sugarcoating the loneliness caused by prophetic untimeliness.

This was the hard lot of most of the Hebrew prophets. Isaiah of Jerusalem was expressly warned by God, "You are not to call hard what this people call hard. . . . It is the Lord of Hosts whom you should hold sacred; he must be the object of your fear and awe." Jeremiah was told similarly, "Brace yourself, Jeremiah. . . . Tell them everything I bid you; when you confront them, do not let your spirit break, or I shall break you before their eyes." Ezekiel's commission was equally stern: "But the Israelites will refuse to listen to you, for they refuse to listen to me; all of them are brazen-faced."

"Why then is my pain unending, and my wound desperate, past all healing?"
—Jeremiah

Some have said that Jeremiah's message was the hardest of all the prophets, a patriot commissioned to speak like a traitor. Others have said his nature was the most sensitive. What we do know is that he reacted with intense feelings of isolation and betrayal: "Because I felt your hand upon me I have sat alone, for you have filled me with indignation. Why then is my pain unending, and my wound desperate, past all healing?" O God, he even complains, "You are like a brook that fails, whose waters are not to be relied on."

God's answer to Jeremiah is severe, almost unsympathetic. "If you turn back to me, I shall take you back. . . . This people may turn again to you, but you are not to turn to them. To withstand them I shall make you strong, an unscaled wall of bronze." Similarly, it was said of Athanasius, the great fourth-century champion of orthodoxy, that he was *"Athanasius contra mundum"* (against the world).

As many lonely and embattled Christians know in our own day, it can be strenuous and demanding to live before the Audience of One. Making unpopular stands or speaking uncomfortable words on his behalf can be painful to the point of anguish.

Time to Get on with It

The second cost of prophetic untimeliness is *a sense of impatience.* For when society becomes godless and the church corrupt, the forward purposes of God appear to be bogged down and obstructed, and the person who lives by faith feels the frustration. At such a moment, untimely people see beyond the present impasse to the coming time when better possibilities are fulfilled. Their response to any delay of the vision is impatience—raw, bit-chomping impatience. And their natural cry is, "How long, O Lord?"

This point is the exact opposite of what is supposed. As the common account runs, anyone who resists the current opinion of the majority or the forward march of the dominant power must be obstructionist. The prevalent trend is progressive, so resistance must be reactionary. Those who don't want to go forward obviously want to go backward. Those who disagree with what the "right" people know to be wise and good are clearly wrong-headed and muddled. You're out of line, they're told. Get out of our way or be crushed by the relentless juggernaut of history.

But such presumption begs the question: To what end, and by what standard? Such words as forward, backward, progressive, and reactionary require criteria and measurement. If what is thought to be right is actually wrong, then clearly it's far better to be "wrong" than "right." If what is held to be progress is in fact going backward or going nowhere at all, far better to go "backward" than "forward."

That is why, as C. S. Lewis pointed out, progress is made by tackling resisting material. The obstinate mass of the status quo may be blocking the progress of truth and freedom. In faith just as much as in science, resistance thinking is anything but reactionary; it is the key to genuine progress.

Once again Nietzsche felt this point keenly. The problem for the untimely person is the frustration of waiting. In his case, however, there was no God to wait for; this earth, this life, and his own endeavors were all he had.

As Nietzsche wrote in *Beyond Good and Evil,* who can stand "the eternal distasteful—'too late!'" To be successful, all we aim for must succeed in time. Therefore without God, waiting "requires strokes of luck and much that is incalculable if a higher man in whom the solution of a problem lies dormant is to get round to action in time—to eruption one might say." In most cases, the lightning of luck does not strike and the waiting is unrewarded, so "in nooks all over the earth sit men who are waiting, scarcely knowing in what way they are waiting, much less that they are waiting in vain."

What makes the frustration worse, Nietzsche continued, is that the call to wake often comes too late.

> [The] accident which gives the "permission" to act—comes too late, when the best youth and strength for action has already been used up by sitting still; and many have found to their horror when they "leaped up" that their limbs had gone to sleep and their spirits had become too heavy. "It is too late," they said to themselves,

having lost their faith in themselves and become henceforth forever useless.

Nietzsche's conclusion is more sobering than encouraging. In the realm of the spirit, the "Raphael without hands"—the genius without the tools to execute his ideas—is the rule and not the exception. In fact, he notes, "Genius is perhaps not so rare after all—but the five hundred *hands* it requires to tyrannize the *kairos,* 'the right time,' seizing chance by its forelock."

> *For followers of Jesus, the* kairos *moment is in God's hands, not ours.*

Is it ever too late to be what we might have been, and to do what we might have done? For followers of Jesus, the kairos moment—the right time in all its fullness of opportunity—is in God's hands, not ours. And this earth, this life, and our endeavors are *not* all we have. So the final End of All Days is assured, and the Days of the Lord that come before then will come again and again and again, as often as God promises or threatens them.

But for those who see those days from afar, and whose faithfulness makes them untimely people in their own age, the wait will still be long and the impatience will still be strong. "How long, O Lord?" will be their cry, and often it will be a cry of pain.

But What Does It All Amount To?

The third cost of prophetic untimeliness is *a sense of failure*. For when society becomes godless and the church corrupt, the prospects of

good people succeeding are significantly dimmed and the tempta-
tion to feel a failure is everpresent. In today's world, this dilemma
confronts us in the form of an added double bind. On the one hand,
we are told by a myriad of Christian speakers that we should be
thinking about our legacy—the clear knowledge of our contribution
after our time on earth. On the other hand, we are told by countless
other Christians that ambition is always wrong; synonymous with
egotism, it is selfish and quite un-Christian.

Both of these positions are wrong. In fact, they are the opposite way around. For as followers of Jesus we can and should be ambi-
tious, but we should never be concerned with our legacies. And the
reason lies in the character of calling.

*Created to be who we are, and called
to be who God knows we can be, we
each reach higher and farther as we rise
to God's call.*

When all that we are, and have, and do becomes a response to
God's call, we live—in Oswald Chambers's famous words—"our
utmost for His highest." Created to be who we are, and called to be
who God knows we can be, we each reach higher and farther as we
rise to God's call. This is the Christian equivalent of the Greeks'
pursuit of excellence—rising to be the very best that we can be. But
"our utmost for His highest" is also the profoundest, the most sub-
lime, and the worthiest ambition that has ever stirred the human
heart.

A simple consequence follows. If we define all that we are before our great Caller and live our lives before one audience—the Audience of One—then we cannot define or decide our own achievements and our own success. It is not for us to say what we have accomplished. It is not for us to pronounce ourselves successful. It is not for us to spell out what our legacy has been. Indeed, it is not even for us to know. Only the Caller can say. Only the Last Day will tell. Only the final "Well done" will show what we have really done.

Those who are called must therefore wait. We can, if we like, thumb our noses at the "bitch goddess of success" and live carelessly when it comes to concerns such as "legacy." But being human, at times this is simply not enough. And just as we want to bring forward the vision rather than hope and trust, so we want to know if we have really succeeded rather than wait for God's "Well done."

Any sense of failure, then, is maddening, for a calling is a project like any venture. And after all, who likes to fail at any task we take on? Yet the truth is that in certain situations and periods of history, failure is only to be expected.

Such a setting is surely the key to understanding God's celebrated words to Baruch, scribe to the prophet Jeremiah: "Do you seek great things for yourself? Do not seek them." This is often taken as a blanket veto on all ambition, but it is more a comment on ambition in Baruch's time—a time of devastation after the fall of Jerusalem to the Babylonians in 586 B.C. In King David's time, or even later in the reign of good kings such as Hezekiah and Josiah, a man of character with ambition might easily have risen to the top of society. But in the grim days of King Zedekiah, evil rather than goodness was fashionable, so there was little scope for good men or women to succeed. The price of faithfulness was apparent failure.

Baruch would not succeed, God tells him, but at least his life would be protected.

How do we each react when we find that our noblest dreams and most profound strivings are staring in the face of failure? Never for one moment must we allow ourselves an excuse to ease up in pursuing God's call. Not for a second can we think of taking the bitter pill of apparent failure and sugarcoating it with rationalizations about the difficult times in which we live.

God knew the times in which he called us to live, and he alone knows the outcome of our times as he knows the outcome of our lives and our work. Our "failures" may be his success. Our "setbacks" may prove his turning points. Our "disasters" may turn out to be his triumphs. What matters for us is that his gifts are our calling.

So every day our work is like a prayer. And every day we give back all we can of God's gifts to him—with love, and trust, and hope.

SIX

ESCAPING CULTURAL
CAPTIVITY

A ND WHAT KNOWS HE OF ENGLAND who only England knows?"
Rudyard Kipling's famous question about British insularity
highlights the issue running through this entire book. If resistance
thinking is so important and untimely people are so vital, where do
we find the counterperspective that frees us from the distortions of
our own situation? How do we arrive at a true perspective from
which to be constructively untimely? How do we establish the van-
tage point from which to resist effectively?

The ancient Chinese cautioned that, because a fish knows only
water, a fish is the last one to ask what water is. But is a better van-
tage point possible for us human beings? Is it something that comes
with the accidents of birth, such as our IQ or the color of our eyes? Is
it something that we stumble on as a serendipity of life? Or is it
something we can learn and cultivate until it becomes a habit of the
heart?

Without God, it must be said, our human knowledge is puny
and perverse, limited on the one hand by finitude and distorted on
the other by sin. All our purely human knowledge is therefore too
restricted and too relative to make us untimely people. Try to become
untimely by your own efforts and you will only succeed in becoming
ornery or a curmudgeon. On top of that, we are all more culturally
shortsighted than we realize.

So there is absolutely no Archimedean point that any of us can reach unaided to give us a fully, finally objective view of life. Unlike the fish, we can walk on land. Unlike the animals, we can fly in the air. And unlike the birds, we can soar into space. But we are still always and only human, and one of the lessons of history is that trying to exceed our human reach makes us not superhuman but inhuman and barbarous.

Without God, our human knowledge is puny and perverse, limited on the one hand by finitude and distorted on the other by sin.

That said, and that said humbly, three things can help us cultivate the independent spirit and thinking that are characteristic of God's untimely people. In ascending order, they are developing an awareness of the unfashionable, cultivating an appreciation for the historical, and paying constant attention to the eternal. Each is crucial for effective resistance thinking.

Awareness of the Unfashionable

The first essential for untimeliness is an awareness of the unfashionable. Nothing sharpens us better for resistance thinking and guards us from slipping into lazy, cowardly thinking than wrestling with truths that are unpopular.

The Challenge of the Difficult

Awareness of the unfashionable is at the heart of C. S. Lewis's 1945 essay on apologetics. Too many Anglican clergy of his day, he said, were teaching what was neither Anglican nor Christian but their own pet doctrines, shaped by popularity and convenience. They were like the false prophets of Isaiah's and Jeremiah's time whose message was audience-friendly to the point of falseness.

The antidote Lewis prescribed was to take "scrupulous care to present the Christian message as something distinct from one own ideas." Anyone who does this, whether an apologist, a preacher, or an ordinary believer, will come up against a bracing experience: "It forces him again and again to face up to those elements in original Christianity which he personally finds obscure or repulsive."

Here, in "the challenge of the difficult," is the secret of resistance thinking. It is too easy to hold or defend beliefs with which we are very familiar, or doctrines that fit in comfortably with the conventional thinking of our day. But if that is all we do, we are likely to find ourselves with a convenient faith that is neither the true faith nor the whole faith. In the words of Captain MacWhirr in Joseph Conrad's *Typhoon*, "Facing it—always facing it—that's the way to get through."

Take the most egregious examples of when the church slipped into Babylonian captivity by accommodating itself to the spirit and system of its times. The Renaissance papacy reflected and became Renaissance power-politics at its purest and most evil. Eighteenth-century liberalism assiduously courted the cultured despisers of the gospel and sired cultured despisers itself. Nineteen-thirties Lutheranism was lured into an affair with German nationalism and

ended up in bed with Nazism. Nineteen-sixties American Protestantism became the secular-chic of its day without any remainder
or any influence. And now, early twenty-first–century evangelicalism
mimics popular culture as closely and successfully as anyone could
ever hope to while still getting away with it. In each case the end
result is not only a betrayal of the faith but a hapless impotence
before the very audience the church was out to impress.

Signs are that, unless some drastic rethinking takes place soon,
the corruptions in evangelicalism will worsen and show through in
theology, not just in practice. Evangelicals have followed the broader
cultural shift from "religion to spirituality" and in the process have
become chronically individualistic rather than corporate; they have
become "do-it-yourself" in their preferences rather than living under
authority; they are increasingly syncretistic rather than exclusive and
discriminating.

What, for instance, would John Wesley or Charles Haddon
Spurgeon have made of evangelicals who read their horoscope as
well as their Bible? How would Jonathan Edwards and D. L. Moody
have responded to evangelicals who believe in reincarnation as well as
the resurrection?

In the name of the most-favored opinions of our modern culture,
some evangelicals have even abandoned the clearest, strongest, most
unambiguous truths about God himself. Some are now trying to
shrink the sovereignty of God, for example, to allow more room for
the vaunting pretensions of free human choice. And many other
evangelicals are too confused or too afraid to challenge such a feck-
less betrayal of faith.

In all such cases, the outcome of extreme accommodation is
such a distortion that the Christian faith becomes unrecognizable

and its power shorn. Lewis's words to liberal Anglicans apply as much to Roman Catholics and evangelicals today: "A 'liberal Christianity' which considers itself free to alter the Faith whenever the faith looks perplexing or repellent must be completely stagnant. Progress is made only into resisting material."

A Radical Obedience

Dietrich Bonhoeffer's stand with the Confessing Church against Hitler shows us a different way. Faced with the appalling sight of Protestant capitulation to national socialism, he stressed the cost of discipleship. He didn't emphasize it as a rational choice based on creedal confession, which clearly could be twisted and harnessed by nationalistic fervor, but as a radical obedience to the call of Jesus, which depended on one thing only—the supreme authority of Jesus, a Lord who outweighed the Führer. The Nazis claimed the allegiance of the whole person, and so did Jesus of Nazareth. Only such a lordship and such a radical discipleship could trump the claims and manipulation of the German state.

> *The Nazis claimed the allegiance of the whole person, and so did Jesus of Nazareth.*

Needless to say, Jesus' appeal in the gospels is as strong as his authority. No one in history has ever been more truly friendly to seekers. His hard sayings are no more the whole gospel than are his comforting sayings. The good news appeals far more than it repels, and it repels only to appeal at a far deeper level.

Overall the gospel is the grandest Yes to human aspirations in all history. But the gospel's No's are plain, unvarnished, and impossible to duck. There is challenge as well as promise, warning of costs as much as offers of rewards, and talk of sacrifice as common as invitations to the party. There is therefore a stern truth in Adlai Stevenson's quip about the distortions of positive thinking: "Paul I find appealing, but Peale I find appalling."

The cross of Jesus runs crosswise to all our human ways of thinking.

In an age when comfort and convenience are unspoken articles of our modern bill of rights, the Christian faith is not a license to entitlement, a prescription for an easy-going spirituality, or a how-to manual for self-improvement. The cross of Jesus runs crosswise to all our human ways of thinking. A rediscovery of the hard and the unpopular themes of the gospel will therefore be such a rediscovery of the whole gospel that the result may lead to reformation and revival.

The Clean Sea Breeze of History

A second essential for untimeliness is appreciation for the historical, for no human perspective gives us a better counterperspective on our own day. For those who do not believe in God or eternity, this is often their only means to guard themselves against the distortions of the present.

> *"Raise yourself on daring wing high*
> *above your own age!"*
> *— Nietzsche to Richard Wagner*

Nietzsche, for instance, writing about his friend, the composer Richard Wagner, exclaimed, "Raise yourself on daring wing high above your own age! Let the coming century distantly dawn already in your mirror!" Or again in *Untimely Meditations*, "One cannot stand out more clearly from the whole contemporary age than through the way one employs history."

The Treasure of Our Mistakes

Are we in good condition to use history to judge the present? The issue is debatable. "Americans renounce history," Jacob Burckhardt wrote, speaking of the way the New World was embraced at the expense of the Old. "History is bunk," Henry Ford said famously in espousing the vast gains of early industrialization. Few would be that blatant today, but the laments about the poor understanding of history are still heard.

Some people decry the present state of history in contemporary culture, pointing to a multitude of factors such as the lamentable teaching of history in schools and a constant obsession in the popular media with the present over the past. Journalist Bill Moyers aptly said of his fellow-countrymen, "We Americans seem to know everything about the last twenty-four hours but very little of the past sixty centuries or the last sixty years."

Others, however, are more encouraged. They cite the growth of local historical associations, the almost insatiable appetite for excellent biographies and histories, and the immense popularity of television series on periods such as the American Civil War and World War II.

But what is not sufficiently appreciated is the fact that historical awareness is one of the greatest fruits of Western (and therefore biblical) thinking. Along with science, history is one of the most striking accomplishments of the Western mind; unlike science, however, it is rarely given the recognition it deserves. The point is far more than a matter of prestige for academic turf battles. The issues behind the importance of history touch on our very character as human beings.

History deals with one-of-a-kind human choices, with accidents, disasters, ironies, and events that are totally unforeseeable and unpredictable.

As John Lukacs has argued in his great reflections on the nature of thinking about history, *Historical Consciousness*, history is essential for our knowledge of ourselves as human beings. Science deals mainly with nature—or ourselves as objects of nature among other objects. But history deals with us, and not as objects but as subjects.

Or again, history is essential for grasping human uniqueness. Whereas science deals with the predictable and the repeatable, with laws and uniform regularities, history deals with one-of-a-kind human choices, with accidents, disasters, ironies, and events that are totally unforeseeable and unpredictable. As Marcel Proust wrote of this feature of our humanity, "Exceptions to the rule are the logic of existence."

If that is true, history provides a deeper and more comprehensive knowledge of our humanity than science does. Lukacs points out, for example, that science is more history than history is science. History is therefore utterly essential to human beings and to human wisdom. At its core, the story of anyone or anything is virtually the person or the thing themselves. The best avenue to understanding the nature of the person or the thing is to tell their story. As Shakespeare says in *Henry V*, "There is a history in all men's lives."

My point is not to advance the imperialism of academic history—I am neither a scientist nor a historian, so I have no dog in that fight. And much academic history is part of the problem, not the solution. What matters to us all, historians or not, is to give history its proper place as an irreplaceable source of human understanding and wisdom.

Santayana's remark that those ignorant of history are condemned to repeat it has been echoed down the ages in countless ways, and needs to be restored to its place in our thinking today.

"Being fond of the truth," Confucius said, "I am an admirer of antiquity."

"Anyone wishing to see what is to be," said Machiavelli, "must consider what has been."

"He who cannot draw on three thousand years," Goethe argued, "is living hand to mouth."

"We learn from the study of history," Hegel wrote, "how mankind has learned nothing from the study of history."

"Man's real treasure," wrote Jose Ortega y Gasset, "is the treasure of his mistakes, piled up stone by stone throughout thousands of years."

Or as Winston Churchill wrote simply in words that go a long way to explain his farsightedness as an unheeded messenger, "The further back you can look, the further forward you can see."

Reading Old Books

Mere lip service to the importance of history will not do. We each have to build in a steady diet of the riches of the past into our reading and thinking. Only the wisdom of the past can free us from the bondage of our fixation with the present and the future. C. S. Lewis counseled, "It is a good rule, after reading a new book, never to allow yourself another new one till you have read an old one in between."

We all have to make our own choices in these things. Some decide to listen to tapes; others choose films and documentaries. Many explore the past through reading richly in the literary classics. I enjoy the classics immensely, but take in my main understanding of history through reading biographies. In tackling a major or minor biography every two or three books I read, I have found my awareness of history steadily expanding along with my appreciation of the colorful throng of men and women who make the human story so fascinating.

Whatever the means you choose, the diet must be steady and the goal clear. Every age has its strengths and weaknesses, its own outlook and blind spots, and therefore its own talent for seeing certain truths and not others. It is essential that we rise above the limitations of being children of our own age.

> *The past is the greatest source of corrective wisdom that helps us to be wise in our own day.*

Second only to the third requirement, our attention to the eternal, an appreciation of history saves us from the various perils of nowism, temporal chauvinism, chronological snobbery, generational conceit, and the parochialism of the present. The past is the greatest source of corrective wisdom that helps us to free us from these mental sins and be wise in our own day. In Lewis's famous words, "The only palliative is to keep the clean sea breeze of history blowing through our minds, and this can be done only by reading old books."

Attention to the Eternal

The third essential for untimeliness is attention to the eternal, for only the eternal is eternally relevant. Simone Weil, the French philosopher, put this with majestic simplicity, "To be always relevant, you have to say things which are eternal."

Breaking into Our Silence

So how on earth—for we are never anywhere but here on earth—can we achieve the impossible? To begin with, we have to face the fact that the pursuit of relevance as being constantly timely is a mirage. When relevance is invoked as a self-authenticating concept, it becomes meaningless and dangerous because it begs the questions, Relevance for what? Relevant to whom?

Such questions are commonly ignored in today's headlong rush after the unholy trinity of the powerful, the practical, and the profitable. But if we don't ask them, the constant appeal to relevance becomes an idol, a way of riding slipshod over truth, and a means of corralling opinion deceptively. Until, that is, we finally deceive ourselves.

Nothing is finally relevant except in relation to the true and the eternal.

The fact is that nothing is finally relevant except in relation to the true and the eternal. Unless something is true, its perspective will at some point be wrong and its practical value in the end will be nil. Only truth and eternity give relevance to "relevance." To think or do anything simply "because it's relevant" will always prove to be irrational, dangerous, and a sure road to burnout. It may taste like unpleasant medicine to our practical modern thinking, but in fact it's a powerful antidote to perpetual folly: There is an irrelevance to the pursuit of relevance just as there is a relevance to the practice of irrelevance.

How then do we lift ourselves above the level of the finite and the mundane to gain an eternal perspective on what is true and relevant? The biblical answer is blunt in its candor. By ourselves we can't. We can't break out of Plato's cave of the human, with all its smoke and flickering shadows on the wall. We can't raise ourselves above the level of the timebound and the earthbound by such feeble bootstraps as reason. But where we are limited by our own unaided efforts, we have help. We have been rescued.

As the story of religion and philosophy shows, our own human explorations—brilliant, profound, and tireless though they have been—never have and never will break out of the silence, whether the numinous final silence of eastern mysticism or the cold, bleak silence of atheism. But we are not left in despair. God has broken into our silence. He has spoken and has come down himself. And in his written and living Word we are given truth from outside our situation, truth that throws light on our little lives and our little world. This word of God is the only effective Archimedean point to gain the leverage to raise us above the forces of gravity in our human condition.

God has broken into our silence. He has spoken and has come down himself.

Yet many believers today are so secular that this point has become a cliché. It seems too spiritual and theological to be practical. But it is precisely in the practical world of global power politics that its relevance can be seen. Long before Soviet Communism fell in 1989, farsighted thinkers pointed out that communism would inevitably fall—by the weight of its own corruptions. This, they stated, was because its ideology had no self-correcting principles. For instance, the eminent social scientist David Martin argued years earlier that, though communism looked much stronger than the Christian church as a force in the world, the church had the seeds of its own self-correction and renewal whereas communism didn't.

One such seed of Christian renewal has been the notion of sin, the church's "doctrine of its own failure." If all of us always go wrong, then corruption is no surprise and correction should be an automatic and needed response. The other seed of correction and renewal has been the church's belief in the word of God, which means that the church always has "a judgment that transcends history." The church may fall captive to this culture or that ideology, to this philosophy or that fashion. But when the Word of the Lord speaks and is listened to, the church wakes up to be herself and the captivity can be thrown off.

When the Word of the Lord speaks and is listened to, the church wakes up to be herself and the captivity can be thrown off.

But people today hear of these seeds of correction and say, not so fast. We now know that if all of our views are conditioned by our cultures, then that also includes our views of the Word of God. In other words, they say, the Archimedean point is once again swallowed up by human relativism. There is no outside perspective.

When even the church's view of the Word falls captive to some mistaken view of the Word, her view is timebound and earthbound again. Such a distorted view will wake up no one; the church will be condemned to perpetual captivity. There is no escape.

To be sure, the danger is real. But this fear confuses the church's view of the Word with the Word itself. God is always bigger than our misunderstandings of him. However distorted and inadequate our views may be, it only takes the real Word to speak to wake up the church and the world. The difference will be clear. Either there really is a Word of God, in which case it is separate from us and our misunderstandings of it, or there isn't and we are shut up once more to the uncertainties of silence.

The church in the West is unquestionably in poor shape today, but this is neither the first time nor will it be the last. Like an eternal jack-in-the-box, the church will always spring back. No power on earth or in the church can keep the gospel down, not even the power of Babylonian captivity and confusion. "At least five times," G. K. Chesterton noted, "the Faith has to all appearances gone to the dogs. In each of these five cases, it was the dog that died."

Puncturing the Ceiling

Recognition of the importance of the eternal is only the beginning. We each have to recover it in our own lives by reinstating it in practical ways.

When I came to faith a generation ago, the practice of daily personal worship was fundamental. We were taught to begin every day with a sustained time of worship, reading the Bible, and prayer. According to the precedent of Isaiah's messianic Servant, we were to practice a regular "morning watch." Only those who hear the word can speak, so those who speak must first have listened ("The Lord God . . . made my hearing sharp every morning, that I might listen like one under instruction.").

In many circles today, however, that habit has worn thin and that practice has become casual. The result is an extraordinary loss for the people of God of a powerful insertion of the perspective of eternity at the very outset of the day.

Equally, when I was young in the faith, regular public worship was considered essential. It was both the practice of the ministers and the expectation of the people that the sermon would bring a direct, helpful, and practical word from God for his people. In many parts of the West this is no longer the expectation or the practice. Church-going is viewed by many as merely optional; an increasing number of people have no regular experience of sitting under an authoritative word from God; and in many parts of the Western world preaching has fallen on very hard times. I have been in megachurches where there was no cross in the sanctuary and no Bible in the pulpit, and where the sermons refer more to the findings of Barna and Gallup than to those of the Bible and God.

The two greatest preachers I have heard are the great Welshman Martyn Lloyd-Jones, of Westminster Chapel, London, and the great Englishman John Stott of All Souls Langham Place, London. Neither of them ever prefaced their sermons with, "This is the word of the Lord." But neither of them needed to. Having prepared before God, come straight from the presence of God, and delivering what they said as from God and in the presence of God, their authority was unmistakable and its effect profound. No prophets could have stirred and challenged their audiences more deeply.

At the same time, there were many more moments in public worship when it was as if the ceiling was punctured and there was an irruption of the transcendent. Did those who lead the worship pray and expect such a breaking-in of the supernatural in ways we no longer do, even with our improved stage management, our choreography, our dance, our drama, and our PowerPoint expositions?

Sometimes the irruption happened during the hymns, sometimes during the preaching, and sometimes during the Holy Communion. It was certainly nothing that was engineered. But it was deep, real, transfixing, and the light it cast would throw the week behind and the week ahead into a different light. When was the last time the ceiling was punctured in your local worship? When was the last time a sermon ended and you just wanted to sit there and ponder what God had just said to you?

We need to practice the presence of God and to pursue the reality of knowing God.

There was many a time when the lightning flash of those moments jolted my heart and mind into seeing things that the normal, secular view never allows. I couldn't begin to say how many of my best ideas have come in the setting of worship. Nothing draws the mind higher than down-draughts of transcendence from the very presence of God.

Needless to say, attention to the eternal assumes and requires the practice of the spiritual disciplines today—to cultivate the spiritual habits of the heart and learn to do as second nature what we cannot do as first. And above all, we need to practice the presence of God and to pursue the reality of knowing God.

The weight, and noise, and pace of modern secular life are almost overwhelming. Only those who desire to know everything of God that a fallen human being can stand to know and still live will be able to keep an eternal perspective and so decide what is truly relevant. For Weil was right: It takes the eternal to guarantee the relevant; only the repeated touch of the timeless will keep us truly timely.

CONCLUSION

FATHER TIME WITH HIS SICKLE, William Shakespeare's "bloody tyrant," John Donne's tolling bell, Charles Baudelaire's "sinister God"—time's many images across the centuries are a stark reminder that, along with the mystery of evil, time is one of the two deepest problems we face as humans. Each has elements that are finally insoluble. They are ultimately too much for our minds to figure out and too great for our ingenuity to outwit. In the case of time, all human life ends. No human success lasts forever. "This too shall pass" is carved over all of our endeavors on this earth.

The human project as a whole begins from a sense of incompleteness and in the case of our little lives, it ends with incompleteness too. There is always more to do. There are always other things we could have done. And in the end, there is always an end. For all the staggering arc of our accomplishments and the soaring reach of our imagination, our reach has a limit. And when we reach that point, we come to the end, and the end of time for all of us is death.

No Way Those Ways

This brief exploration into the crazy world of modern time is only a tiny footnote to the age-old story of our human grappling with time as a whole. But to set things in their wider context serves as a bracing reminder. If over the centuries we haven't found a solution to defeating time, then today we are unlikely to come up with a solution to a problem that the modern world has only made worse.

One thing is clear: The false and inadequate answers are more obvious than ever. For instance, some people try to arrest time through nostalgia—a focus on the past accompanied by a desperate homesickness for a vanished time and world. But nostalgia tells us less about home and more about the distance we have come and the headlong speed we are traveling. Its attempts to revive memories of a happier time are usually both understandable and harmless. But they do nothing to bring us home. They say nothing about our prospects of ever coming home. And they do not slow down time by one single second.

A second response some resort to is the idea of eternal recurrence, or an Eternal Return. The fleeting present may have no meaning because of its transience, but if it comes around again and again, it is not forever lost and may gain meaning beyond what we can see now. But eternal recurrence just transfers the problem of meaninglessness from one place to another. Nietzsche made this move in *Will to Power* when he argued that "everything seems worth too much to be so fleeting; I am searching for an eternity for everything. . . . My comfort is that everything that was is eternal—the sea washes it back again."

What this really shows, however, is how little meaning there is "under the sun" for the secularist in the purely secular span of things when "God is dead." It underscores the conclusions of Ecclesiastes and switches us from Western secularism to eastern pantheism or monism. But it doesn't show how the endless cycle of things, with all its resignation and fatalism, makes the situation any better or more meaningful.

The third attempted solution is today's favorite answer to the challenges of time—better time management and improved efficiency. Increased gadgetry, better planners, and a more efficient use of time may certainly lead to a better use of time, and thus to greater productivity. But that leads only to an even faster pace of life and to even greater pressures.

> *The rat race speeds up, but it's still a race for rats.*

Have we forgotten why we went to the time-and-motion experts in the first place? The rat race speeds up, but it's still a race for rats. We're scrambling faster and faster, and our multitasking now has the dexterity of a twenty-armed Indian god. But all we're doing is getting ourselves more and more mired in the devouring quicksand of time.

Redeeming the Time

False answers, however, are not the last word. Those who worship the Lord of time and history, who disclosed himself to us on Sinai and in Galilee, can draw three positive conclusions.

First, we may say with all the certainty of Scripture and the evidence of history that the secret of integrity in a world obsessed by time and the future is to be untimely. Two hundred years after the Enlightenment, the monumental price of blind faith in progress is undeniable. The simple-minded tendency to indict the past and laud the future is folly. As C. S. Lewis pointed out in *The Screwtape*

Letters, most vices are associated with the future—for example envy and lust—whereas the virtue of gratitude has to do with the past and the virtue of trust with the present.

The prototype of all future-fixated talk was Lincoln Steffens's remark after coming back from the Soviet Union, "I saw the future and it worked." His comment proved as foolish as his vision proved disastrous, and many who gush with similar promises for the church will be equally disappointed.

Far better the wisdom of John Lukacs, "I saw the future and it was the past." Or his version of the old French aphorism, "What is most alive in the present is the past." For the fact is, 99 percent of what we know about the future is the past. Far better too the astuteness of Billy Graham who, when criticized for "setting the church back fifty years," answered that he was sorry he had not set it back two thousand years.

To those who say we cannot turn the clock back, the answer is that, when we need to, we do it every year. And in the deeper case of the church of Christ, that setting back of the clock means reformation and revival. To go forward, the church must always first go back.

To go forward, the church must always first go back.

Second, we may also say with certainty that, in a world obsessed with change and progress, progressives will always prove stagnant while resistance thinkers will be fresh and creative. Striving for incessant motion, those with a mania for change will only achieve frenzied movement, preoccupation with trifles, and in the end wasted energy and exhaustion. By contrast, resistance thinkers will move things forward constructively.

Was St. Augustine "reactionary" in his massive defense of the church against her pagan critics in *The City of God* in the fifth century? Undoubtedly, but he was also years ahead of his time, with views of governance and time, for example, that have yet to be plumbed or superseded. Was Blaise Pascal "old-fashioned" in replying to the sophisticated skeptics of his day in the seventeenth century? Yet his *Pensées,* even though unfinished, are as fresh as the day they were written, whereas most of the works of his contemporaries are of antiquarian interest only.

There is even a good reason why wisdom may increase with age, a point worth noting in a culture obsessed with youth. As we get older our reflexes are slower and our powers of retention smaller, and we certainly have no more idea now of what the future may hold. But a large part of wisdom comes from the accumulated experience of knowing what the future will *not* hold, and that vital wisdom increases as we get older. In other words, comprehension and wisdom improve even as memory falters. Wisdom is a matter of the *quality* of what we know, not the *quantity.*

Third, we may also say with certainty that in a world dominated by the tyranny of time, the only final way to redeem the time is through the one who is the redeemer of everything. The shining story of the success of clock time conceals an irony. Invented to help us escape nature, the clock has left us enslaved by the machine. Thus to free ourselves from the tyranny of time through using more mechanized solutions is to load more chains onto our captivity—or to punch the tar baby harder and harder and stick more firmly than ever.

Philosophers are right. Deep down, time isn't really money. The dirty secret is that money is really time. We spend, or use up, our time in making money; we spend time in spending money; and we even spend time in hoarding money. Time is our final currency in life, and all the money in the world can't give us extra seconds, minutes, or days. When we think of the craziness of life, we say that the world is too much for us; but when we think of the tyranny of time, we realize the world is not enough for us.

"In Heaven," novelist Kurt Vonnegut wrote, "you can be any age you like." But not down here. Time isn't impressed by honors, awards, or bank accounts. It isn't fooled by cosmetics and plastic surgery, or even by exercise. The sickle keeps sweeping closer. The sands in the hourglass are fewer by the second. One day the bell will toll for each one of us. And that is when our views of time and life will matter, for their truth or falsehood will make the difference in that day. What price nostalgia or time-and-motion experts then?

How then do we redeem time, and how are we redeemed from time? On the one hand, we redeem the time by living out our lives according to our gifts and callings, thus serving God's purposes in our generation. Those who live out their lives in this way do justice to the best of their time; and they live before all time because they live before God.

On the other hand, we redeem time by trusting the end of our time to the Lord and redeemer of time. Ultimately, we redeem the time and are redeemed from time only through the one who is the redeemer of everything—He who *is*, the God who is the Lord of time and history and yet is "the same yesterday, today, and forever."

In St. Augustine's description, God relates to us in time in ways that are "once for all [*semel*], all at once [*simul*], and always [*sem-*

per]." He is before our time, outside our time, and at the end of our time. We can therefore each pray Augustine's celebrated prayer, which applies to time as much as any part of life: "You have made us for yourself, and our hearts are restless until they find their rest in you."

Thus until the day of our homecoming arrives, we continually trust that the Lord of time will redeem us at the end of time. And in the meantime that is our lives, we live out our callings in the thick of things, and so set about redeeming time actively though imperfectly, as timely as untimely people can ever be.

O God our help in ages past, our hope for years to come,
Our shelter from the stormy blast, and our eternal home:
Under the shadow of thy throne thy saints have dwelt secure:
Sufficient is thine arm alone, and our defence is sure.

Before the hills in order stood, or earth received her frame,
From everlasting thou art God, to endless years the same.
A thousand ages in thy sight are like an evening gone;
Short as the watch that ends the night before the rising sun.

Time, like an ever rolling stream, bears all our years away;
They fly, forgotten as a dream dies at the opening day.
O God, our help in ages past, our hope for years to come,
Be thou our guide while life shall last, and our eternal home.

—Isaac Watts

FOR FURTHER READING

Daniel J. Boorstin, *The Discoverers: A History of Man's Search to Know his World and Himself* (New York: Random House, 1985).

Eva Brann, *What, Then, Is Time?* (Lanham, Md.: Rowman & Littlefield, 1999).

John Lukacs, *Historical Consciousness: The Remembered Past* (New York: Schocken Books, 1985).

Dietrich Bonhoeffer, *The Cost of Discipleship* (London: SCM Press, 1948).

Dallas Willard, *The Divine Conspiracy: Rediscovering our Hidden Life in God* (San Francisco: HarperSanFrancisco, 1998).

Louise Cowan, Os Guinness (eds.), *Invitation to the Classics* (Grand Rapids, Mich.: Baker Book House, 1998).

ACKNOWLEDGMENTS

This little book is written with grateful thanks to Dr. Stan Mattson and the C. S. Lewis Foundation, whose invitation to contribute to Oxbridge 2002 was the genesis of this book; to Richard King Brown, Eric Metaxas, David and Suzy Young, George and Lucy Marsden, Nigel and Gillie Goodwin, Norman Stone, Ranald Macaulay, Gregory and Frederica Mathews-Green, and Mary Elizabeth Warren, Shawn Plunkett and friends, who made the week so delightful as well as stimulating; to Amy Boucher Pye, whose gifts as an editor are now legendary in my world; and to Jenny and CJ, whose love and support have been invaluable to a crazy writer who, every so often, can't get certain ideas out of his head.